LIVING IN ...
ANCIENT GREECE

LIVING IN...
ANCIENT GREECE

Series consultant editor: Norman Bancroft Hunt

CHELSEA HOUSE
PUBLISHERS
An imprint of Infobase Publishing

LIVING IN ANCIENT GREECE

Text and design © 2009 Thalamus Publishing

Chelsea House
An imprint of Infobase Publishing
132 West 31st Street
New York, NY 10001

Library of Congress Cataloging-in-Publication Data

Bancroft-Hunt, Norman.
  Living in ancient Greece / Norman Bancroft-Hunt. — 1st ed.
    p. cm. — (Living in the ancient world)
  Includes index.
  ISBN 978-0-8160-6339-0
  1. Greece—Civilization—To 146 B.C.—Juvenile literature. I. Title. II. Series.

DF77.B257 2008
938—dc22

                                    2008009475

Chelsea House books are available at special discounts when purchased in bulk quantities for businesses, associations, institutions or sales promotions. Please call our Special Sales Department in New York at (212) 967-8800 or (800) 322-8755.

You can find Chelsea House on the World Wide Web at: http://www.chelseahouse.com

For Thalamus Publishing
Series consultant editor: Norman Bancroft Hunt
Contributors: Roger Kean, Angus Konstam, Warren Lapworth
Project editor: Warren Lapworth
Maps and design: Roger Kean

Printed and bound in China

10 9 8 7 6 5 4 3 2 1
This book is printed on acid-free paper

Picture acknowledgments
All illustrations by Oliver Frey except for – Jean-Claude Golvin: 22-23, 26–27, 29 (bottom), 65, 76–77; John James/Temple Rogers: 56–57 (top); Roger Kean/Thalamus: 2, 5, 12–13 (all), 20, 25 (both), 36 (inset), 41 (top), 47 (plate), 48 (both), 56-57 (all pots/panel), 63 (top, all 6), 73 (top right), 76 (bottom right), 80 (center), 88 (top left); Mike White/Temple Rogers: 3, 28 (left), 28–29 (bottom), 32 (bottom, all 4), 33 (top and center), 36 (main), 42 (top), 44-45 (top), 46 (top), 63 (bottom).

Photographs – Archivo Iconigrafica/Corbis: 24, 60, 85; Dave Bartruff/Corbis: 77; Christies Images/Corbis: 41; Corbis: 8; Gianni Dagli Orti/Corbis: 23, 59 (right), 61 (top and centre), 76 (bottom, 78 (bottom), 84 (bottom) Kevin Fleming/Corbis: 37; Mimmo Jodice/Corbis: 21 (left), 59 (top); Daid Lees/Corbis: 22 (inset); Francis G. Mayer/Corbis: 59 (bottom); Vanni Archive/Corbis: 29, 78 (top); Roger Wood/Corbis: 59 (left), 84 (top)

CONTENTS

Place in History

6000 BCE
4000 BCE
3500 BCE
2340 BCE
1900 BCE
1600 BCE
1100 BCE
539 BCE

MESOPOTAMIA

3100 BCE
2686 BCE
2200 BCE
2040 BCE
1782 BCE
1570 BCE
1070 BCE
747 BCE
332 BCE
30 BCE

EGYPT

2600 BCE
1100 BCE
800 BCE
500 BCE
146 BCE

GREECE

753 BCE
509 BCE
27 BCE

ROME

476 CE

800 CE

1200 CE

1350 CE

1450 CE

MIDDLE AGES

At the Dawn of Democracy

In a long and glorious history, ancient Greece gave the world a wonderful legacy of art and literature. The invention of an alphabet that allowed for the development of sophisticated prose and poetry led to the invention of the theater and complex drama. Western art reached its peak as Greek sculptors created the first truly lifelike statues and their architects developed a style of public building that has lasted until today. The Greeks also invented coinage as a means of payment, but above all, they established a form of government that today we call "democracy." Thanks to the Greeks the voice and will of the people is paramount in government.

Landscape and Climate

Few civilizations in the ancient world were as much a product of their geography as Greece. Three-quarters of Greece is mountainous, and only one-fifth of the land can be cultivated.

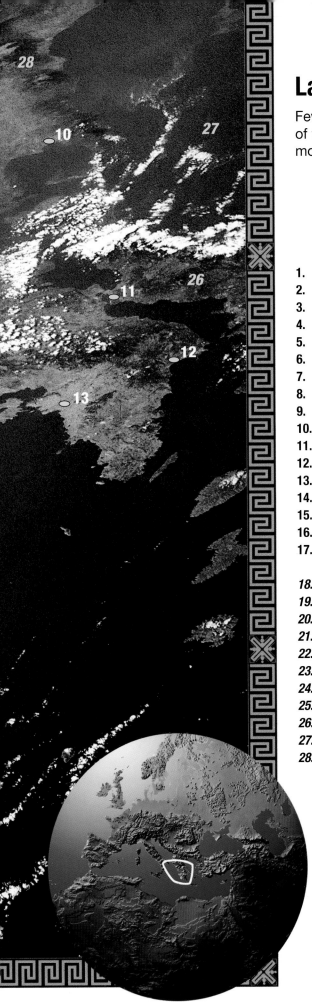

1. Nicopolis
2. Olympia
3. Pylos
4. Sparta
5. Epidaurus
6. Thermum
7. Patra
8. Delphi
9. Thermopylae
10. Iolkos
11. Chalkis
12. Marathon
13. Athens
14. Corinth
15. Mycaenae
16. Argos
17. Tiryns

18. "Heel" of Italy
19. Corfu
20. Cephalonia
21. Zante
22. Cythera
23. Ionian Sea
24. Sea of Crete
25. Gulf of Corinth
26. Euboea
27. Aegean Sea
28. Mount Olympus

Most land suited to agriculture is found along the coastal plains and in a few area of the Peloponnese. Within the sparsely populated mountainous interior, many communities were isolated from each other, and even more so from the more inhabited coastal regions. This isolation led to societies that developed in very different ways.

Climate, too, played a role in increasing social isolation. Mountain passes, blocked by snow in the extremely harsh winters, cut off communication even between neighboring valleys for several months of the year. The spring melt made the few tracks impassable for a further period.

With pastoral land rare, the great plain of Thessaly was the only place for raising horses, which made Thessalians the strongest in cavalry. For much of the rest, travel and battling on foot was the norm.

The Spartan heartland in the Eurotas valley of the Peloponnese was very fertile, but it was a cradle surrounded by the crags of Lakedaimon. As a result of their location Spartans developed as a proud and fiercely independent race, but also domineering and, as their population expanded, territorially aggressive toward other Greek nations.

Athens, on its protective gulf, surrounded by sea, naturally developed as the dominant seafaring nation. Athenian traders became the logistics carriers for the region, although many other seaside cities also used the sea as a means of communication.

A look at the map of Greece shows the many long fingers of land and islands, so it is no wonder the Greeks became the most adventurous of Mediterranean sailors after the Phoenicians. The poor quality of their land forced many Greeks to leave their mainland homes and seek lands overseas to settle—the Aegean islands, the coast of Asia Minor (modern Turkey), Sicily, southern Italy, and even as far off as southern France. In Sicily, Greeks and Phoenicians would battle for supremacy over many centuries.

A History of Greece, 2600–146 BCE

A patchwork of small, fiercely independent city-states, constant inter-city warfare prevented national unity and eventually weakened the Greeks, who fell to external threats.

While the Stone Age tribes of mainland Greece were beginning to establish primitive urban settlements, on the island of Crete a great Bronze Age civilization arose, known as Minoan. Centered on the great city-palace of Knossos, Minoan Crete flourished between 2600 and 1250 BCE, exporting its culture throughout the southern Aegean.

The civilization began to decline after 1628 through a series of disasters. First the volcanic island of Thera (modern Santorini) exploded, sending a massive tidal wave to crash into the northern shore of Crete. War with the mainland Mycenaeans eroded wealth and an invasion of the Sea People, who later attacked Egypt, and then the Dorians fatally weakened the Minoans.

Mycenaean heroes

The Mycenaeans (named after their most important city of Mycenae) were Indo-Europeans who migrated into Greece in 1900–1600 BCE. With a knowledge of horses and bronze technology, the Mycenaeans soon made the inhabitants of the scattered Greek settlements their subjects.

Most cities of the time were derived from Mycenae—Sparta, Thebes, Athens, and Pylos being the most important. Mycenae was the home of Agamemnon, the high king who led the Greeks across the Aegean Sea to make war on Troy. Along with them went the legendary heroes of Homer's *Iliad*, men like Achilles, Ajax, and Odysseus. Troy was destroyed in about 1200, when Mycenae was at its peak. By this time, an early form of Greek writing had been established.

The Sea Peoples who destroyed the Minoans are also blamed for the collapse of the Mycenaean age, but there was another wave of invaders called Dorians, who may have been a part of the Sea Peoples or another Indo-European race altogether. What is certain is that by 1100 BCE Greece was plunged into a Dark Age.

The Dark Age lasted 300 years, during which time Greece remained a mysterious and barbaric land, a patchwork of small settlements, each ruled by a "barbarian" Dorian warlord.

Troy wins out

Romans claimed descent from the survivors of Troy, who fled to Italy after Greeks destroyed their city. An irony, then, that "Trojans" came back 1100 years later as Romans to steal Greek freedom.

By 800 BCE, things had settled down, trade returned, and small independent city-states sprang up. New iron technology brought improvements in farming tools and weaponry. Agriculture improved dramatically, paid for by the cities, which in turn jealously protected the immediate countryside about them. The time between 800 and 500 is generally called the Archaic Period.

This was also a time when the great migrations of colonists began to settle along the coasts of the Black Sea, in Sicily and southern Italy, and along the North African coast. Colonies expanded trade, and the accumulation of wealth promoted the birth of the Classic Period of Greek history.

War and the development of politics

The ancient Greek word for "city" is *polis*. A *metropolis* is a "mother city," and politics is the business of governing a city-state. Most Greek cities were still ruled by warlords, but Athenians experimented with other types of government. "Oligarchy" was government by a self-elected council of *aristoi* (aristocrats). Sometimes the *aristoi* chose a single man to rule, called a "tyrant."

However, this concentration of power irritated the growing mass of wealthy citizens, who had no say in the government but yet were expected to supply the men

Below: This reconstruction shows the city of Mycenae at its peak in the 13th century BCE. The large building in the center is the *megaron*, or throne room of the palace. Mycenaean buildings used massive stones in their construction, a style called "cyclopean" by later Greeks. They believed that men could never have raised such heavy blocks and instead these cities were built by the giant one-eyed cyclops.

and arms for the numerous petty wars with other city-states.

Eventually, by 510 BCE internal strife and a war with Sparta brought power to the *demos* (people). Except for Sparta—which retained its kings—the other Greek cities soon adopted democracy, or "rule by the people" (*see pages 70–73*).

War with Persia

In 490 BCE, the expanding Persian Empire under Darius I invaded. Because of war with Sparta, Athens stood alone to face the threat. A band of 10,000 Athenians defeated twice as many Persians at the battle of Marathon.

Darius died in 486, and his son Xerxes—delayed by events in Egypt—attacked in 480 with a vast army. This time Sparta sent 300 soldiers, who held the Pass of Thermopylae for days before they were cut down. Their bravery bought time for Athens to ready its fleet. In the great sea battle of Salamis, Athens trounced the Persians and broke the back of the invasion. Sensing victory, all the Greek states joined in and decisively defeated Xerxes at the Battle of Plataea in 479.

Athens and Greece fall

Athens now became the premier city of Greece, using its wealth to erect some of the finest temples and public buildings ever seen, including the Parthenon. But austere Sparta hated its rival and war broke out in 431. The Peloponnesian War lasted until 404, eventually dragging in most cities on one side or the other. In the end, worn out, Athens fell to Sparta's military might.

The war had devastated Greece and paved the way for the rise of Macedon. Under first King Philip II and then his son Alexander, Macedon conquered Greece. Alexander went on to conquer the Persian Empire and found a series of Hellenistic (Greek) dynasties that fragmented after his death in 323. Further power struggles continued to reduce Greece, and even Macedon was unable to resist the new power in the Mediterranean—the Romans.

Philip V supported the Carthaginian general Hannibal against Rome, and in return the Romans invaded in 171 BCE. By 146, all of Greece was under Roman domination, and thereafter it would remain a province of the Roman Empire.

Table of Major Dates

	3000	2000	1500	1000	800

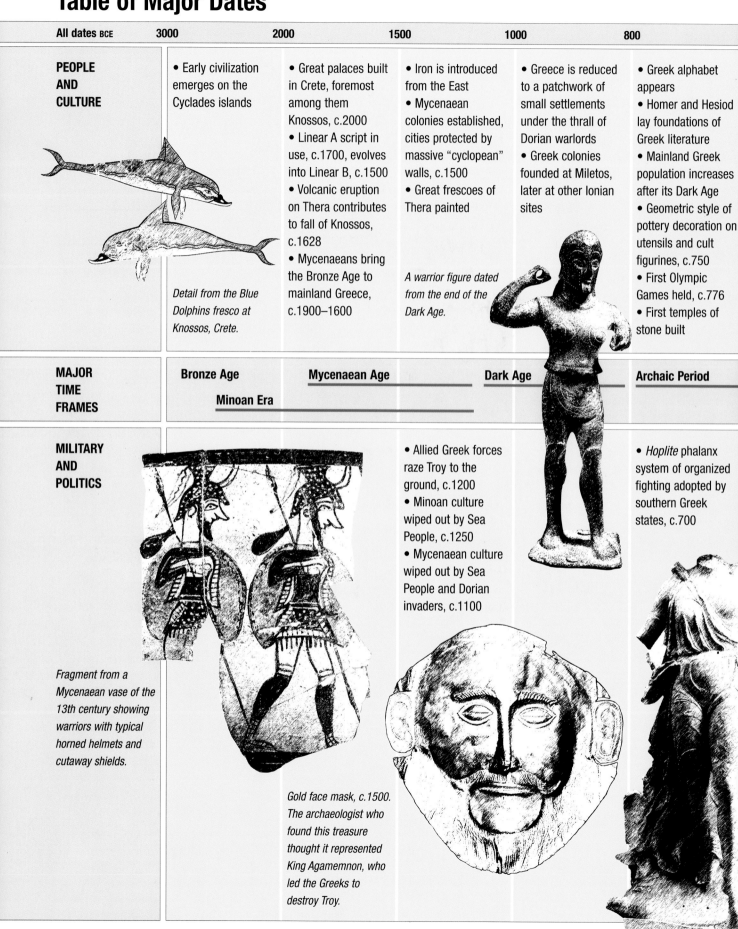

PEOPLE AND CULTURE

- Early civilization emerges on the Cyclades islands

Detail from the Blue Dolphins fresco at Knossos, Crete.

- Great palaces built in Crete, foremost among them Knossos, c.2000
- Linear A script in use, c.1700, evolves into Linear B, c.1500
- Volcanic eruption on Thera contributes to fall of Knossos, c.1628
- Mycenaeans bring the Bronze Age to mainland Greece, c.1900–1600

- Iron is introduced from the East
- Mycenaean colonies established, cities protected by massive "cyclopean" walls, c.1500
- Great frescoes of Thera painted

A warrior figure dated from the end of the Dark Age.

- Greece is reduced to a patchwork of small settlements under the thrall of Dorian warlords
- Greek colonies founded at Miletos, later at other Ionian sites

- Greek alphabet appears
- Homer and Hesiod lay foundations of Greek literature
- Mainland Greek population increases after its Dark Age
- Geometric style of pottery decoration on utensils and cult figurines, c.750
- First Olympic Games held, c.776
- First temples of stone built

MAJOR TIME FRAMES

Bronze Age   Mycenaean Age   Dark Age   Archaic Period

Minoan Era

MILITARY AND POLITICS

Fragment from a Mycenaean vase of the 13th century showing warriors with typical horned helmets and cutaway shields.

- Allied Greek forces raze Troy to the ground, c.1200
- Minoan culture wiped out by Sea People, c.1250
- Mycenaean culture wiped out by Sea People and Dorian invaders, c.1100

Gold face mask, c.1500. The archaeologist who found this treasure thought it represented King Agamemnon, who led the Greeks to destroy Troy.

- *Hoplite* phalanx system of organized fighting adopted by southern Greek states, c.700

500	400	300	200	100	AD

- Greek coins begin to appear
- City-states increase in power
- First *kourai* and *korai* (boy and maiden) statues appear
- First black-figure decoration on pottery
- Dramatic choral plays are introduced at Athens

- Aischylos introduces first written play, c.490
- Age of Pericles
- Thinkers and writers include: Euripides, Herodotus, Socrates, Thucydides, Aristophanes, Plato, and Aristotle
- First red-figure decoration on pottery
- Temple of Zeus constructed at Olympia

- Praxiteles the sculptor astonishes with his lifelike work
- Mausoleum of Halicarnassus constructed

Coin showing Alexander wearing the ram's horn of Egyptian god Amun.

- The Altar of Zeus is erected at Pergamum
- Statue known as Venus de Milo is the peak of neo-Classical style
- Winged Victory (Nike) sculpted for Samothrace
- "Hellenistic baroque" style reaches Petra in the kingdom of Nabataea

---

- Greek literature, philosophy, sculpture, and architecture begins to influence the Romans
- Despite his hatred of the Hellenizing influence, Porcius Cato the Elder constructs the first Greek-style basilica in Rome, c.184

Athenian orator Demosthenes railed against Alexander.

- Greek prose writer and historian Plutarch born near Thebes, 46

Classic Period | **Hellenistic Period** | **Roman Empire**

- Beginnings of democracy in Athens
- Sparta is the dominant power of the Peloponnese

Statue of Nike (Victory) erected near the Temple of Zeus at Olympia by the allies of Athens in celebration of their defeat of the Spartans at the battle of Sphakteria.

- Persian invasions under Darius I (490) and Xerxes I (480) are thrown back
- Slave rebellion in Sparta, 464
- First part of Peloponnesian War starts, 461–451
- Second part of Peloponnesian War starts, 431–404
- Athens defeats Sparta at Sphakteria, 425
- Argive League dissolved by Sparta, 418
- Athens' fleet is defeated by Chios, one of the island states in revolt against Athens, 411
- Besieged and starved, Athens surrenders to Sparta. 404

- Athenian revival
- Athens and Corinth fight Sparta in the Corinthian War, 395–386
- Philip II comes to power in Macedon, 359
- Macedon defeats Athens and Thebes at Chaeronea, 338
- Alexander succeeds Philip and reimposes his will on Greece, 336
- Alexander begins conquest of Asia Minor, 334
- Alexander conquers Egypt, found Alexandria, c.331
- Alexander dies at Babylon, leaving behind a series of warring Hellenistic "Successor States," 323

- Ptolemaic, Seleucid, and Antigonid successor states battle for supremacy in Asia Minor, Thrace, and Greece
- Celtic Gauls invade Greece in 279, later settled in Galatia in Asia Minor
- Macedonian Wars, 214–205 and 200–196, bring greater Roman influence to the region

---

- Rome declares war on Macedon in retaliation for its support of Hannibal, 171
- Macedon becomes a Roman vassal, 168
- The Achaean League opposes Roman influence in the Achaean War, 147
- Roman forces defeat the league's army between Thebes and Athens, then march on Corinth and destroy the city; Achaean League dissolved and Greece declared a Roman province, 146

Head from a portrait statue of Philip II of Macedon, father of Alexander the Great.

- King Mithridates VI of Pontus massacres 80,000 Romans in Asia Minor and frees most of southern Greece from Roman rule, 88
- Roman general Sulla defeats Mithridates, burns Athens, ransacks Greek shrines, and demands reparations for rebellion, 86
- Caesar's adopted son Octavian and Mark Antony defeat Republican forces in Macedonia. Antony makes Athens his capital, 42
- Ptolemaic Egypt becomes a Roman province after the death of Cleopatra, last Greek queen, 30

CHAPTER 1
Land of Gods and Heroes

From the Beginning of Time

In a time before real Greek history came to be written down, there was a golden age, when gods and heroes walked the earth alongside ordinary mortals.

Before the creation of the world, there was only Chaos. From Chaos emerged Gaia the mother—first of the Titans, gods and giants who ruled the earth before their overthrow by Zeus. Without mating, Gaia produced a son called Uranus, who represented the heavens. Gaia then mated with Uranus and they had many Titan children. These included Rhea and Cronus (Father Time), who came to rule after defeating Uranus.

Cronus and Rhea had many children, but fearing for his own position, he ate them all as they were born, until Rhea tricked him into eating a rock instead of the newborn Zeus. Later, Zeus rebelled against Cronus and made him disgorge all his siblings. Then he banished Cronus and the other Titans to the Underworld.

Other important Titans

Meanwhile, Oceanus (oceans) and his sister Tethys produced the rivers and 3000 water nymphs, while Hyperion married his sister Theia, who gave birth to Helios (the sun), Selene (moon goddess), and Eos (the dawn).

Iapetos married a nymph and fathered Prometheus (god of forethought and wisdom), Epimetheus (god of afterthought and stupidity), and Atlas. Unlike his brothers, Atlas supported Cronus against Zeus, and when Zeus won he punished muscular Atlas by making him support the world on his back. Zeus then ordered Prometheus and Epimetheus to create humankind.

The sky gods

These are the Greek myths of the creation. But myths always represent some sort of reality. The overthrow of the Titans (the earth gods) by Zeus and the Olympians (the sky gods) represents a major change in

After the titanic struggles, Zeus emerges as the ruler of all the gods. From the cloud-capped summit of Mount Olympus, he is assisted by an extended family, an inner circle of 11 other Olympians (*shown here in the family tree, with their roles listed overleaf*).

14

prehistoric Greek society. The original natives of Greece worshipped the female-ruled earth gods, but the Indo-European Dorians—who invaded from the north in about 1100 BCE—worshipped the male-dominated sky gods called Olympians.

Later Greek writers explained this change by reorganizing the way the pantheon (collection of gods) worked. They say that Zeus drew lots with his brothers, Hades and Poseidon, to become supreme ruler. Zeus won, and became ruler of the sky, Poseidon received the seas, and Hades ended up in the Underworld, to rule over the dead.

From this time onward the Olympians were the brothers and sisters of Zeus, as well as his children born of many goddesses and nymphs, including his sister and jealous wife Hera.

Jealous and bad-tempered gods

The Greeks believe the sky gods dwell on top of sacred Mount Olympus, from which they get their collective name. But the family is riven with jealousy. In the myths, the Olympians are always arguing and use mortals to help them get their way.

This interference in human affairs brings benefits but also great dangers to the favored person, who is almost certain to earn the enmity of another god or goddess as a result. During the Trojan War, Zeus took the Greeks' side, while Apollo favored the people of Troy, and almost all the gods interfered in the adventures of Odysseus.

So, the Greek gods are not necessarily benign, and accounts of their plotting and treachery make it clear that they suffer from all the common sins of humanity—only on a grand scale. Given the gods' erratic and often bad-tempered natures, Greeks spend more time in their temples trying to keep them happy than they do hoping to follow their divine example.

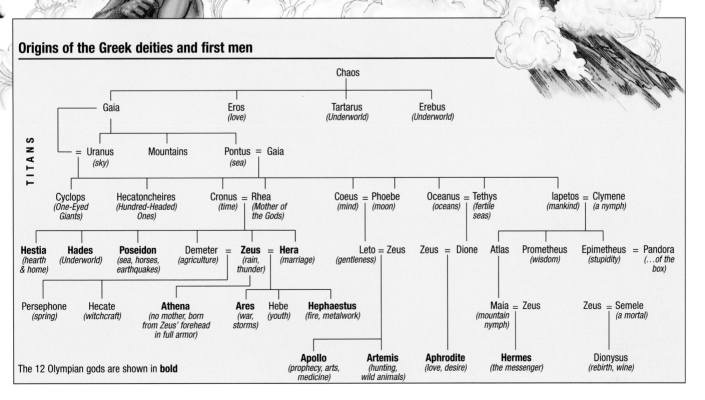

Origins of the Greek deities and first men

The 12 Olympian gods are shown in **bold**

Roles of the Olympian Gods

The number of Greek divinities is staggering—someone to look after every aspect of life, occasion, and event. Here are the primary roles of the Olympians; lesser gods appear throughout this book, accompanied by a brief description.

Hera: marriage, birth

The wife of Zeus is always jealous of his many love affairs. She punishes her rivals and their children with terrible fury. Zeus—who rarely stands up to her—resorts to trickery, by hiding his children or changing them into animals to disguise them.

Poseidon: sea, earthquakes

As god of the sea, sailors pray to him for a safe voyage—but he is not always reliable. In a bad mood, Poseidon strikes the ground with his trident and causes earthquakes and storms, shipwrecks and drownings. Among his numerous children are the half-human and half-fish Triton, the flying horse Pegasus, and (according to some) Theseus, a king of Athens.

Athena: war, wisdom, arts, justice

It is said that Zeus feared that his first wife Metis, goddess of wisdom, might bear a son mightier than himself, so he ate her. Inside, she began making a cloak and a helmet for her daughter. The hammering caused Zeus great pain and made him cry out. At that Hephaestus split his father's skull open and from it emerged Athena, fully grown and wearing Metis's robe and helmet.

Athena contested her uncle Poseidon for a certain city they both wanted. He made a well spring up, but the salty water did not please the people. Athena's gift was an olive tree, which gave the citizens oil, wood, and food. So they acclaimed her the winner and named the city after her—Athens.

Apollo: music, prophecy, medicine, poetry

Apollo is identified with Helios the sun god. He is also the god of plague—according to Homer's *Iliad*, Apollo shot plague-infected arrows into the Greek camp in the Trojan War. His most important cult center is at Delphi, which he occupied after slaying a dragon called the Python. He then dedicated the sanctuary and gave oracular powers to a priestess—the Pythia—to whom people go to seek answers to the future. One of his sons is Asclepius, the god of healing (*see page 86*).

Artemis: hunting, wild animals, fertility

Her main role is to hunt lions and wild game in the forests, attended by her nymphs, and armed with a bow and arrows made by Hephaestus. Artemis is quick to punish any man who insults her. When a young hunter accidentally saw Artemis and her nymphs bathing in a pool, she turned him into a stag. Then she set his own dogs on him and, thinking he was just another stag, they chased and killed their master.

Hermes: messenger and herald of the gods

Hermes is also patron of literature, weights and measures, merchants, shepherds, athletes, thieves, and travelers. In this last guise he looks after roads and boundaries, which is why the marker stones at intersections and frontiers are called "herms." Athenians place herms outside their houses to fend off evil. As a herald, it is also his duty to guide dead souls to the Underworld; and while they sleep he brings dreams to mortals.

Hephaestus: fire, metalworkers

Hephaestus is the patron of all craftsmen, especially those working with metal. He is also the god of volcanoes. He is known as the lame god, because he was born weak and disabled. Hephaestus makes weapons and armor for the other gods and heroes, as well as the thunderbolts Zeus throws. He also made the sun chariot in which Helios rides every day across the sky.

Ares: war and destruction

Where his ugly brother Hephaestus is kind, handsome Ares is vain and cruel. He enjoys bloody battles, with little care for which side wins—the other gods dislike Ares almost as much as they do Hades.

Aphrodite: love, desire, beauty

She was so beautiful that Zeus married her to Hephaestus, the steadiest of the gods, to keep her in check. But Aphrodite, who enjoys laughter and glamor, is not pleased at being the wife of hard-working Hephaestus. She is loved by many gods and mortals. Her festival is the Aphrodisiac, celebrated in many centers. Aphrodite is associated with the Mesopotamian Ishtar.

Hestia: the hearth fire, domestic life

Hestia swore to remain a virgin. She has no throne, but tends the sacred fire in the hall on Olympus and every hearth on Earth is her altar. She is the gentlest of all the Olympians. The Romans call her Vesta.

Hades: ruler of the dead and the Underworld

Hades has a helmet which makes him invisible. He rules the dead, helped by his assistants, the ferryman Charon and the three-headed hound Cerberus. Because everyone's wealth finally comes to Hades, he is referred to as "the Rich One." Of all the gods, Hades is the one who is liked the least, even by the gods. He abducted Persephone from the upperworld to be his wife.

Major temples and sanctuaries in the Greek homeland

🏛 Mt. Olympus (Zeus, all gods)
🏛 Dodona (Zeus)
LESBOS
🏛 Pergamum (Athena)
🏛 Delphi (Apollo)
🏛 Lebadea (Trophonius)
🏛 Eleusis (Demeter)
🏛 Nemea (Zeus)
🏛 Isthmia (Poseidon)
🏛 Clarus (Apollo)
🏛 Olympia (Zeus)
🏛 Delos (Apollo)
🏛 Didyma (Apollo)
RHODES 🏛 Lindos (Athena)
CRETE 🏛 Mt. Dicte (Zeus)

Trophonius (Lebadea) is a son of Apollo and an early Greek oracle.

Zeus was born on Mount Dicte.

Greek Heroes

The heroes of Greek mythology stand between the gods and mortals. These cult figures include real warriors as well as those of legend. In a world where the deities' example is not necessarily one to follow, they are an inspiration to ordinary people.

The origins of the hero cult lie in the 10th century BCE, and are associated with the development of a particular part of Greece, such as Heraeus, founder of the city of Heraea (from which the word "hero" is derived).

Greek mythology contains many accounts of the actions of gods, goddesses, nymphs, and satyrs, but the central characters are usually heroes. Many of them are the children of the gods, or at least of royal parents particularly blessed by the gods. Although they are raised above common mortals, they share their human lifespan.

Heroes in the Trojan War

Through the writings of Homer (in his *Iliad* and *Odyssey*), most of these heroes are associated with the Mycenaean era (ended by about 1100 BCE). This is the period of the Trojan War, when King Agamemnon of Mycenae led a fleet and army to besiege the city of Troy (Ilium to the Greeks), on the far side of the Aegean Sea.

Agamemnon's companions are the ultimate Greek heroes—warriors such as Achilles, Ajax, Menelaus, Nestor, Diomedes, Philoctetes, and Odysseus. They are matched by the heroism of their Trojan rivals—Priam, Hector, and Paris.

As an infant, Achilles had been dipped in a sacred pool whose waters made him invincible, save for the heel by which his mother held him. Helen, Spartan wife of Menelaus, was reputedly a child of Zeus, as was her brother Pollux. The goddess Athena protected Odysseus on his post-war travels.

Tales of fate and irony

The Greeks believe in this blend of heroism and divinity because the characters are historic to them. They had lived only a few centuries earlier, and in the same part of the world. The place names mentioned by Homer are real and can be visited by any Greek traveler.

The common theme in these tales is fate. On returning from the Trojan War as heroes, they are still unable to escape their mortal fate. Agamemnon is murdered by his wife in a palace coup when he returns to his capital. Odysseus spends ten years wandering the seas trying to get back home, only to have to kill his wife's new suitors, after she had given him up for dead.

This notion of irony and fate is a continual theme, from the tale of King Oedipus of Thebes (who, through a confusion of events, unknowingly kills his father and marries his mother), or Icarus, the son of Daedalus, to Theseus, who slays the Minotaur. The blend of moral statement, heroic deed, and revenge over enemies and unfaithful partners binds the Greeks to their heroes—superhuman, and yet mortal.

The fate of Icarus

The inventor Daedalus built the labyrinth that housed the monstrous Minotaur of King Minos of Crete. But when he helped the hero Theseus of Athens to kill the Minotaur and escape the maze, Minos imprisoned Daedalus and his son Icarus. Unable to escape the island by sea, Daedalus used his skills to build wings for himself and Icarus. Daedalus warned Icarus to fly at moderate altitude. Too high and the sun might melt the wax fastening the feathers to the wings— too low and the sea might dampen the feathers.

Alas, young Icarus, excited by the flight, ignored his father's warning and flew ever higher and higher. The sun melted the wax and the boy fell into the water and drowned.

The myth explores a favorite theme of a man attempting to equal the gods and suffering retribution for his presumption and arrogance. It also points out that the young often suffer for ignoring their parents' wisdom and experience.

Jason and the Argonauts

King Pelias of Iolcos, fearing Prince Jason's ambition, sent him on an impossible mission to bring back the fabled Golden Fleece from distant Colchis. Jason and his crew—the Argonauts—sailed off in their ship, the *Argo*. On the voyage, they became the first humans to pass through the Clashing Rocks.

In order to receive the fleece, the king of Colchis demanded that Jason plow a field using fire-breathing oxen and sow it with the teeth of a dragon. Then he must defeat the warriors who spring from these "seeds." Finally, Jason had to overcome the sleepless dragon who guards the fleece.

He was helped in these deeds by Medea, the king's daughter. After obtaining the Golden Fleece, the two fled back to Iolcos, where Medea murdered King Pelias. Later, Jason deserted her for another woman. Medea took her revenge by murdering the bride and her children. Jason was killed years later when a piece of timber from the *Argo* struck him on the head.

This myth describes the probably real coup that took place at Iolcos when the half-legendary King Jason came to power there. But it mingles with the earliest accounts of Greek traders who ventured through the Hellespont strait (the Clashing Rocks, known today as the Dardanelles) into the Black Sea, where Colchis was supposedly situated. The irony of Jason's fate is that his famous ship kills him.

Achilles' heel

Achilles, son of the mortal Peleus and the nymph Thetis, was the mightiest of the Greek heroes in the Trojan War. Thetis made her baby immortal by dipping him in the River Styx, whose sacred waters make everything it touches become invulnerable. But she held him by one heel, which remained dry and unprotected. Years later, in the war, Achilles distinguished himself by many deeds and was recognized on both sides as an undefeatable warrior. However, when Paris, son of the Trojan King Priam, shot Achilles in the unprotected heel with an arrow, Achilles died of the wound.

Fate, it seems, is inescapable, even for the greatest of heroes.

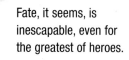

Oracles and Mystery Cults

Religious festivals are often the only break from daily routine that most citizens enjoy, so they are widely popular. They allow the free population of a city to join together for religious devotion and civic entertainment.

In a civilization with so many gods to please, festivals are common. Religious observation in Greece is virtually a constant activity, since to omit the worship of a god is to invite divine retribution—and no one wants that.

To an outsider, many of these festivals might appear far from religious. They include events such as panhellenic (all-Greek) athletic games (*see pages 74–77*), theatrical dramas (*see pages 90–93*), and civic processions designed to please those taking part and those watching. But every one is dedicated to the gods and held in locations that have a religious significance for the Greeks. Many of these have been dedicated to one or more of the Olympian deities.

And all festivals are linked to a certain mystery cult, or the worship of a particular god or goddess.

One of the most mysterious of cults is that of the Pythian oracle of Apollo at Delphi. This red-figure painting on a plate shows a king consulting the priestess Pythia at Delphi, seated on her three-legged "tripod" stool.

The big festivals

Most religious festivals begin with a procession, where the god's cult followers honor their deity, while other citizens with their wives and children—gather on the sides to offer observance. Those in the procession carry food offerings for the god, such as honey, bread, and cake. Sometimes livestock is slaughtered in a sacrificial ritual. Dancing and singing often feature in these events, which can last for several days.

Large cites like Athens, Thebes, and Corinth hold several festivals every year, and even larger events every two, three, or four years. The most famous of these is the Athenian Great Panathenaic procession, a week-long festival held every four years in honor of the goddess Athena.

A United Nations of Greece

Most cults are local affairs, but several festivals unite all of Greece. These "panhellenic" festivals are often held in locations of particular religious importance, such as at Delphi (dedicated to the god Apollo) or Eleusis (cult center for Demeter). These sites are lavishly provided with festival buildings, temples, and sports stadiums.

Here, especially during festivals, the sacred ground is neutral, so even warring city-states may meet each other in safety. Their delegates can even discuss peace or trade treaties. Almost every city-state of Greece has its treasury on the grounds of Delphi because the gods' scrutiny provides security.

Demeter and Eleusis

One of the oldest cults is that of Demeter, the goddess responsible for the earth's fertility, particularly the growth of cereal crops. She ended mankind's nomadic existence by teaching the skills of plowing and sowing. Her cult center is at Eleusis, a complex some 14 miles northwest of Athens with the great temple of Telesterion at its heart. It has grown over centuries, as the plan opposite shows.

Wisdom of the oracle

The most famous oracle in Greece is that of Apollo at Delphi (*see also pages 22–23*). It was discovered long ago that a cleft in the side of Mount Parnassus emitted a gas that caused seizures among the goats that grazed nearby. When a goatherd was also affected, the locals interpreted his convulsions and ravings as divine inspiration.

This became the place decreed by Apollo to be the *omphalus* (navel) of the world. Delegations now travel from all over Greece to seek advice, the words of Apollo interpreted through the medium of the Pythia, high priestess of Delphi.

The Pythia is crowned in laurel and seated on a tripod perched over the vaporous cleft. Any man (women are not allowed in the sanctuary) wishing to ask a question about the future must first be ritually purified by washing in the Castalian Spring, which is where Apollo killed the Python dragon.

The request is written down and given to the Pythia by a priest. Her utterances are usually so disjointed that her servant-priests are needed to interpret the answer—even then, they often get it wrong, to the questioner's usually dreadful misfortune.

Worship and fun

Since most cults are limited to men, the festivals of Dionysus (god of wine) are popular, since women may also take part. The festivals involve drinking a great deal of wine, mass chanting, and frenzied dancing (*see also page 41*).

The antics of the Dionysian cult may not look like worship, but celebrating their gods through festivals is an important part of Greek religious belief. And while they celebrate, they are also free from the constraints of normal daily life, which makes Greek festivals a unique combination of devotion, entertainment, and spectacle.

Right: The Pythia, seated on her tripod, goes into a trance to utter the words of Apollo.

Left: The worship of Demeter is based on the mysteries of natural cycles.

Eleusis

800–500 BCE
500–350 BCE
350 BCE – CE 300

acropolis

sanctuary gates
lesser   greater
propylaea   propylaea

N

sanctuary of Hades
treasury
Megaron (throne room)
Temple of Kore

houses

triumphal arch

Temple of Artemis

terrace

6th-century walls

Telesterion

4th-century walls
"sacred house"

Sacred Way

Sacred Way

fountain
baths
triumphal arch

gymnasium

cisterns   Periclean walls
(5th century BCE)

0   150ft
0   50m

A Day Out at Delphi

Delphi is located on the southern slopes of sacred Mount Parnassus, about 12 miles from the Gulf of Corinth. While some come here to question the oracle, most attend the site to celebrate a festival of Apollo or Dionysus.

This reconstruction shows the entire Delphi complex, from the stadium at the top to the Sanctuary of Athena at the very bottom-right. The area of the plan is indicated in red.

The celebrant climbs a steep road toward the sanctuary entrance at its eastern corner. During a major festival this road is lined by numerous stores selling the pilgrims food, mementoes of their visit, and sacrificial offerings to place on the many altars. From the gate, the Sacred Way rises steeply in a zigzag, between the votive altars and then the state treasuries of several city-states.

It takes a sharp bend in front of the Athenian treasury before passing close to the rock on which in ancient times the mythical prophetess Sibyl sang her predictions in Gaia's shrine. From here, the procession continues up past the Porch of the Athenians. This *stoa* (a covered walkway) is built in the Ionic order, and has seven fluted, or grooved columns, each made from a single stone. According to the inscription, it was erected by the Athenians after 478 BCE to house the trophies taken in their naval victories over the Persians.

The Sacred Way now bends around to take the last, steep rise up to the great Doric temple dedicated to Apollo. Inside is the *adyton*, the seat of the Pythia.

Facing the steps to the temple's entrance is the large altar of the sanctuary. It was paid for and erected by the people of Chios, in the 5th century BCE. The monument is made of black marble, except for the base and cornice, which are of white marble, resulting in an impressive color contrast.

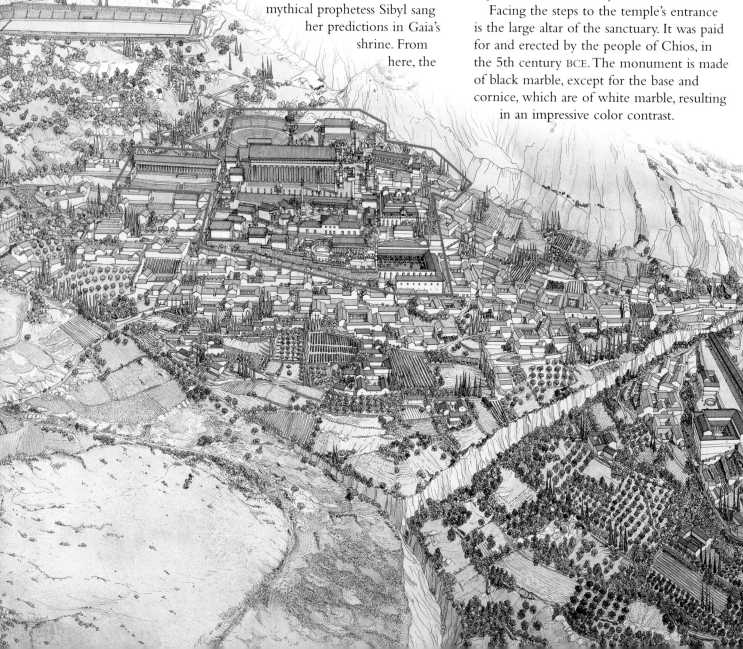

Drama and recreation

In addition to the many altars, Delphi has a large theater with 35 rows of stone benches, where dramatic performances associated with the cult of Dionysus are given. Beyond it, just outside the wall, is the large stadium where the panhellenic Pythian Games take place.

Outside the southwestern wall stands the *gymnasium*. This complex of buildings is used by the youths of

Delphi for their education and athletic practice. It is constructed on two levels, with a free open space used for running practice on the upper, and on the lower a *palaestra* (exercise yard), the pool, and the *thermae* (baths).

All these many and varied activities form a part of the experience of visiting Delphi.

The theater is an important part of the religious activities.

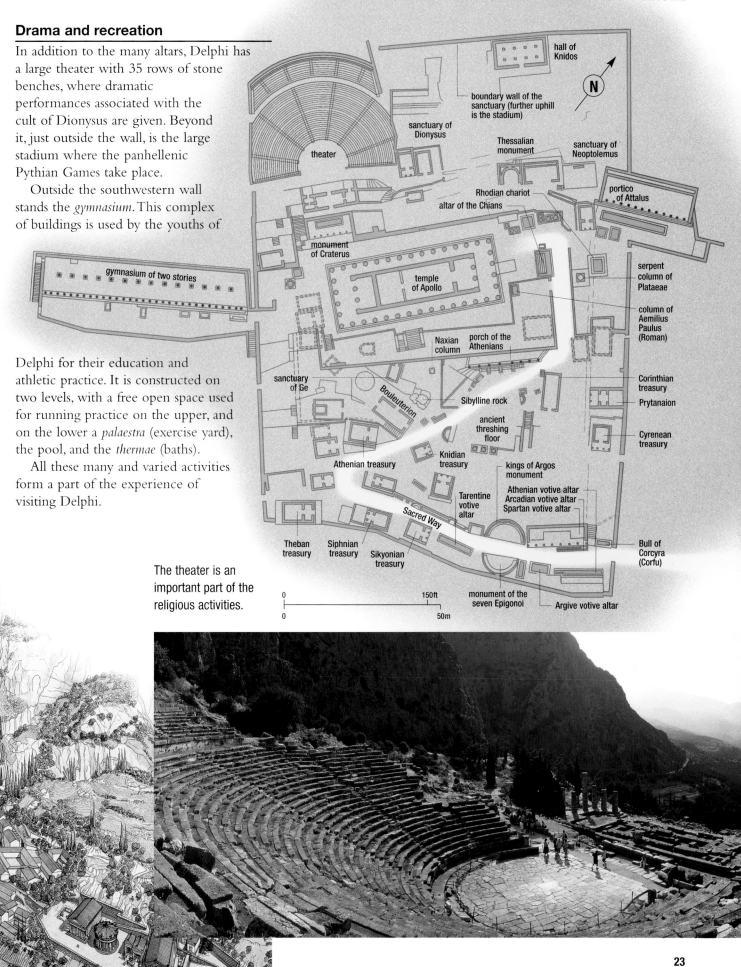

hall of Knidos

boundary wall of the sanctuary (further uphill is the stadium)

N

sanctuary of Dionysus

theater

Thessalian monument

sanctuary of Neoptolemus

portico of Attalus

Rhodian chariot

altar of the Chians

monument of Craterus

serpent column of Plataeae

column of Aemilius Paulus (Roman)

temple of Apollo

Naxian column

porch of the Athenians

gymnasium of two stories

Corinthian treasury

Prytanaion

sanctuary of Ge

Bouleuterion

Sibylline rock

ancient threshing floor

Cyrenean treasury

Athenian treasury

Knidian treasury

kings of Argos monument

Athenian votive altar
Arcadian votive altar
Spartan votive altar

Tarentine votive altar

Sacred Way

Bull of Corcyra (Corfu)

Theban treasury

Siphnian treasury

Sikyonian treasury

monument of the seven Epigonoi

Argive votive altar

0 ———— 150ft

0 ———— 50m

The Greek Temple

The temple is the greatest expression of civic Greek pride. A temple is the house of a god, so much attention is given to building and decorating it.

In Greek worship, the main focus for the celebrants is the altar. In its earliest form, the altar was little more than a simple block of stone standing in the open air. This explains why, even at great religious centers like Delphi, there are so many altars—small and large—standing within the sanctuary without the protection of a building. Even when a temple is erected, its associated altar is placed outside to the east of it and not inside the building (*see the plan on the previous page, altar of the Chians*).

The temple itself is designed to be an *oikos* (house) for the god's cult statue. The basic plan of the earliest Greek temple was based on the ground plan of a house, and grander temples based on a Mycenaean palace *megaron* (throne hall). Like a simple house, these temples consisted of a *cella*, or single room, with porches at the front supported by columns. To distinguish the divine house from a mortal one, the temple was made longer, with the cult statue placed at the back of the *cella*.

Temples become more elaborate

Later temples have a peristyle, an outer series of posts supporting extended roof eaves. This colonnade provides a covered ambulatory (roofed walkway) and distinguishes the building from purely civic architecture. All these early temples were constructed of wood, or from mud brick, with timbering and a thatched or clay tile roof.

After about 650 BCE, the Greeks began to visit Egypt regularly and saw the monumental stone buildings there. This

The Tholos (a round temple) which stands outside the sanctuary of Delphi is a 4th-century monument with a circular peristyle surrounded by 20 Doric columns.

inspired Greek architects, and they began to replace their simple wooden pillars with stone columns, architraves, and cornices. However, they retained much of the original wooden structure in the new stone forms—so the *triglyphs* represent the ends of wooden beams (*see Parthenon diagram, right*).

In time, three distinctive styles of columns, and the capitals that topped them and supported the roof, evolved. The three types of arrangement are called "orders" and known as Doric, Ionic, and Corinthian. The earliest, Doric, is simple and severe in appearance, while the latest, Corinthian is very elaborate in its decoration.

Doric style

The Doric order arrived in the later seventh century BCE. Its parts—simple, baseless columns (fluted or plain), spreading capitals, and the *triglyph-metope* frieze (alternating

Below: The three Greek orders of architecture. Only the capitals (tops) are relevant, the columns are for display purposes. Although earlier columns are plain, later designs are usually fluted.
A) Doric—severe and plain.
B) Ionic with volutes.
(C–E) Corinthian, showing the increasing complexity of decoration, with acanthus leaves as the common form of adornment.

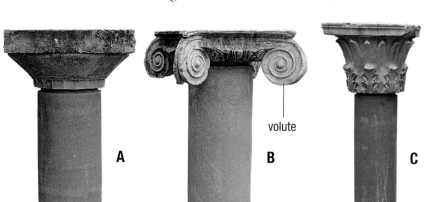

volute

A   B   C   D   E

Reconstruction of the west end of the Parthenon

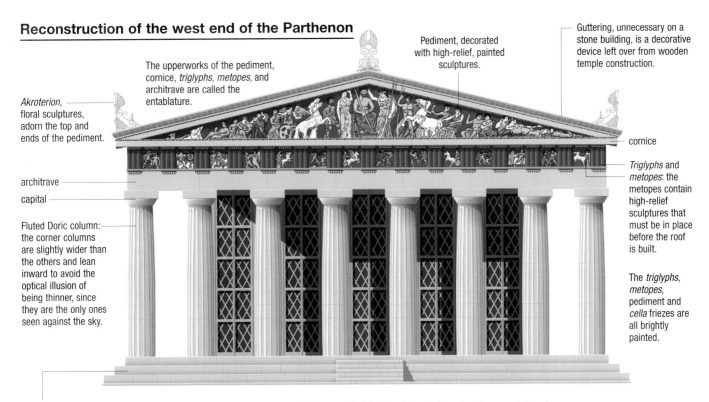

The upperworks of the pediment, cornice, *triglyphs*, *metopes*, and architrave are called the entablature.

Pediment, decorated with high-relief, painted sculptures.

Guttering, unnecessary on a stone building, is a decorative device left over from wooden temple construction.

Akroterion, floral sculptures, adorn the top and ends of the pediment.

cornice

architrave

capital

Triglyphs and *metopes*: the metopes contain high-relief sculptures that must be in place before the roof is built.

Fluted Doric column: the corner columns are slightly wider than the others and lean inward to avoid the optical illusion of being thinner, since they are the only ones seen against the sky.

The *triglyphs*, *metopes*, pediment and *cella* friezes are all brightly painted.

Stylobate: traditionally, three steps all around. It is not flat—like the columns, the architects use tricks to avoid the illusion that long, straight platforms appear to sink in the middle, so each curves upward as it nears its center. The long sides are 4.3 inches higher and the east and west ends 2.3 inches higher.

This west end of the temple is not the main entrance—that is at the east end, with the altar beyond it. The room behind the doors seen here guard the Delian treasury, the funds raised by the Greek island allies of Athens to fight their common enemies.

vertically ridged and plain blocks) above the columns—are an aesthetic development in stone of the structures used functionally in earlier wood and brick construction. Doric has long remained the favorite order of the Greek mainland and western colonies, and has hardly changed throughout its history.

Ionic order

The Ionic order evolved later in about 600 BCE, in eastern Greece. While the basic proportions and construction style of Doric is retained, columns with capitals elaborately carved in floral hoops, known as "volutes" distinguish the Ionic style—borrowed from oriental models.

Corinthian order

The most slender and ornate of the three Greek orders, Corinthian is characterized by a bell-shaped capital with its double row of carved acanthus leaves, and an elaborate cornice. The earliest example dates from about 420 BCE, but the Greeks themselves make little use of the Corinthian style—although the Romans love it.

The Acropolis of Athens

The most impressive examples of Greek architecture of the high Classical Period were built on the Athenian Acropolis for Pericles. The Acropolis architecture—while it is a clear display of civic pride—shows subtlety of design in the use of the Doric and Ionic orders. The Athena Parthenos, or Parthenon—designed in the Doric style by the sculptor Phidias and architects Ictinus and Callicrates—contrasts with the Erechtheum. This temple, which houses several cults, provides a decorative Ionic counterpart to the severe Parthenon.

The Parthenon is the cult house for a great statue of Athena by Phidias, a statue that honors the city goddess; the oldest cult of Athena is housed in the Erechtheum.

Columns are never straight. To avoid the "slimming" illusion that tall, straight sides give, they bulge outward by about an inch one-third of the way up, and are narrower at the top than at the base (the effect is exaggerated in this illustration).

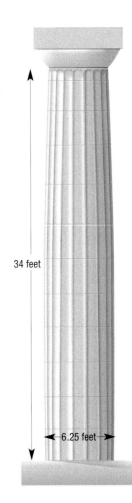

34 feet

6.25 feet

The Great Panathenaic Festival

This festival takes place every four years in Athens. It is the grandest in all of Greece, matched in importance only by the Olympic Games.

The "all-Athenian festival" is one of the occasions when women can get out of the house and take an active role in a public function. Even *Metics* (foreign residents) and freed slaves may participate in some of the festival's events. The holiday starts on the last day of the first month of the Athenian year, which is Athena's birthday. It lasts for a whole week, and brings great joy through the ahtletic and musical contests, sacrifices, feasting, and the great procession.

Proof of fitness and skill

The contests include athletics, music, singing, equestrian events, torch relay races, and boat races. The last are not a usual part of Greek festivals, but the citizens honor Athena's association with boat-building (she helped construct Jason's ship *Argo*). The various types of athletic competition are covered in the section on the Olympics (*pages 74–75*).

All these events, except for the torch and boat races, are open to boys (aged 12–16), *ageneios*, or youths (16–20), and men. The first- and second-place winners receive jars filled with olive oil as prizes. The olive tree and its fruit are sacred to Athena (*see page 16*) and the oil is a valuable commodity almost anywhere in the world. Prize-winners usually sell their oil for cash.

In three cultural competitions, contestants show their musical ability in singing while playing on the stringed *kithara* or the *aulos* (a reed woodwind instrument), while *aulos* players perform without singing. Winners of these contests are also well rewarded. The *rhapsodes* ("stitchers of song") are also highly prized. These are not singers, but reciters of epic poetry, particularly Homeric poems.

The Panathenaic procession

This is the festival's highlight. Starting before dawn, the procession proceeds along the Panathenaic Way through the *agora* (*see page 64*) toward the Acropolis, stopping only for sacrifices offered on the Areopagus hill.

1. The Panathenaic Procession approaches the Acropolis from the Areopagus hill (off to the left of the picture).

2. Only Athenian citizens may enter the Acropolis precinct up the great ramp which leads to…

3. The *propylaea*, or monumental gateway.

4. Athena's giant statue.

5. *Erechteum*, named after a legendary Athenian king.

6. The Parthenon.

At the Acropolis only Athenian citizens may climb the ramp to pass through the monumental gateway called a *propylaea*.

The focus of the procession is in front of a small templed called the Erechtheum, where a newly woven *peplos* (a traditional woman's garment of the Archaic Period) is placed on the giant statue of Athena, guardian of the city. The *peplos* is so large that it has to be carried on the mast of a ship on wheels. The parade concludes with a huge animal sacrifice at Athena's altar, followed by a banquet of meat, bread, and cakes.

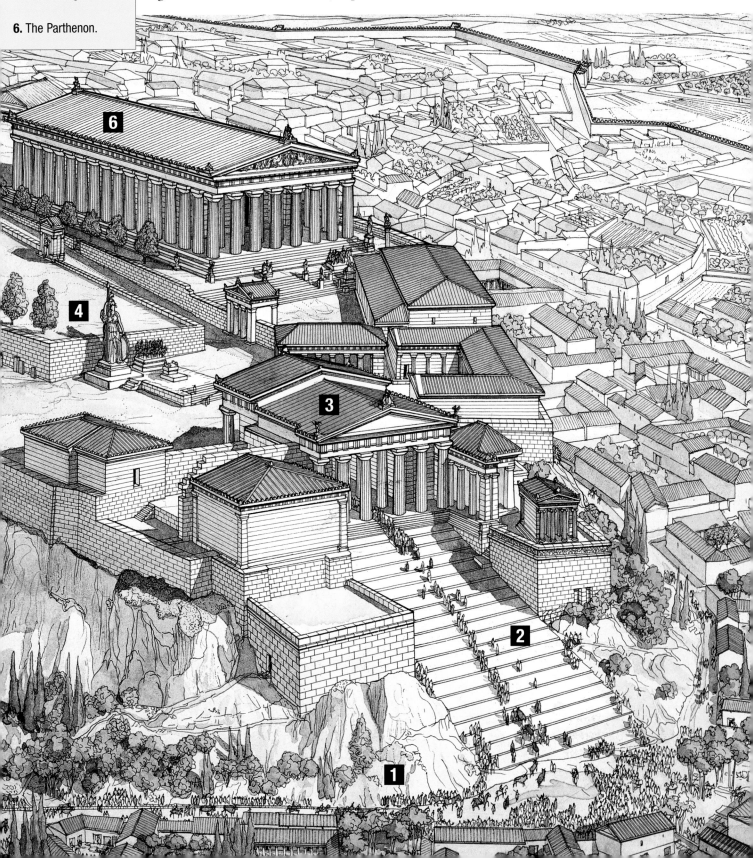

Death and the Underworld

Unlike the Egyptians, who believe in reanimation of the deceased, the Greeks see death as one of the harsher lots of mankind, and the Underworld a shadowy place populated by disembodied souls.

When a person dies, their shade (spirit) leaves the body to enter the kingdom of Hades, god of the dead. What is left behind is just a phantom image, which must either be buried or cremated—wealth generally decides the choice. Slaves are simply buried in small pots, and few poor people can afford a cremation.

Since women usually own little in the way of property, their funerals are simple affairs, but a man must prepare carefully for his death. As soon as a man senses his end is near, he makes out his will. Failure to do so may result in acrimonious lawsuits among his family. Because widows rarely inherit, the will details who will look after his wife and daughters. It says how his wealth is to be shared among the male family members and may mention certain favorite slaves to receive freedom. It gives directions as to the style of his tomb and finally names those he wants to execute (carry out) the will's instructions.

Above: A sensible man makes sure his will is in order, to avoid family squabbles over his property after his death.

Above: After paying their respects, people wash their hands before leaving the deceased's house because death is thought to be unclean.

Preparing for the funeral

As soon as the physician has declared a man dead, the women of his family take charge of the body. It is important to place a coin in the deceased's mouth to pay Charon the ferryman, who will take the soul across the River Styx to enter the realm of Hades. Those who do not pay are stranded on the shores of the Styx and may come back to haunt their families—not an appealing prospect.

The body is washed in perfumed water, clothed in festal white, and the head crowned with vine leaves. Now, properly dressed for the funeral, the body is laid out on a couch in the front doorway of the house, with the face turned toward the street to greet anyone who comes to pay their last respects.

Dead souls pay Charon the Ferryman to row them across the River Styx to Hades' kingdom, also known as the Underworld. The three-headed dog Cerberus guards the entrance to the Underworld.

A funeral procession makes its way toward the prepared pyre.

A noisy lamentation

A wealthy Greek man expects to receive elaborate funeral rites, and in some cities it has become necessary to limit the amount spent, otherwise great sums may literally "go up in smoke" on the funeral pyres.

The mourning is loud and protracted. The widow beats her breast, tearing her hair (unless she has already shaved it off), while the other women sprinkle ashes on their heads. By contrast, when a man buries his wife, the behavior is more restrained.

In the background, the slave women keep up a loud moaning and even the visiting men shed tears and utter loud lamentations. Outside, the hired dirge singers maintain a melancholy chant, beat their breasts, and almost convince passersby that they are frantic with grief.

The funeral procession

Because a person's shade cannot enter the Underworld until all the funeral rites have been completed, it is essential to proceed with the funeral by the second day after death. This is held as early as possible in the morning, before sunrise.

Male relatives carry the funerary bier, following behind the hired dirge singers. The corpse has a honey cake put in his hands and a flask of oil placed under their head. The grieving widow, chief heir, and other male relatives follow the bier. Women under the age of 60 are not allowed to join a funeral procession unless they are first cousins or closer kin of the deceased.

The procession takes a long time, not only because it proceeds at a slow pace, but because the cemetery is placed along a main road beyond the city walls.

The burial

At the appointed place, a funeral pyre is already prepared. There are no priests present, no prayers are said or hymns sung. The ashes are placed in a small urn and buried. Later, a simple stone monument may be erected above the urn or coffin, and on the third, ninth, and 30th days after the funeral there are simple religious ceremonies with offerings of garlands, fruits, and offerings of wine at the new tomb.

Greek funerary monuments are usually restrained in size and appearance. Depictions of the deceased are graceful and often tender. On this *stela* (marker stone) a son is seen fondly greeting his father. At the opposite end of the scale from the modesty of most Greek funerary monuments is the Mausoleum at Halicarnassus (now Bodrum in Turkey). Built to house the body of the tyrant Mausollus of Caria and completed in 350 BCE, the outer walls are filled with statues. The burial chamber sits on a pillared podium, topped by a pyramid-shaped roof. On its summit, a marble statue of a chariot pulled by four horses dominates the structure.

CHAPTER 2

Living off Land and Sea

Ownership of the Land

Greece is divided into numerous small city-states that claim ownership of the surrounding countryside. Within each state, most citizens are farmers, but what they own is dictated by their wealth—or lack of it.

Three-quarters of Greece is mountainous, rocky and barren, and only one fifth of the land can be cultivated, as the map below shows. Despite this drawback, most people in Greece make their living from farming. Even the citizens of towns often have a farm in the country to provide their main income.

The best farming land is found around the coastal plains, parts of Attica, and in Thessaly.

However, with hot and very dry summers, the main crops are called "Mediterranean"— ones that thrive on winter rainfall and need no rain in the summer. These crops include wheat, barley, grapes, pomegranates, figs, and olives.

Rural areas are often very isolated, with communities separated from their neighbors by steep ridges and mountains. Here, life can be poor, with farmers producing only enough food for their own needs. Nearer to the sea, the better quality land provides a wider variety of foods, as well as a plentiful sea catch and products imported from elsewhere, especially cereals from Egypt.

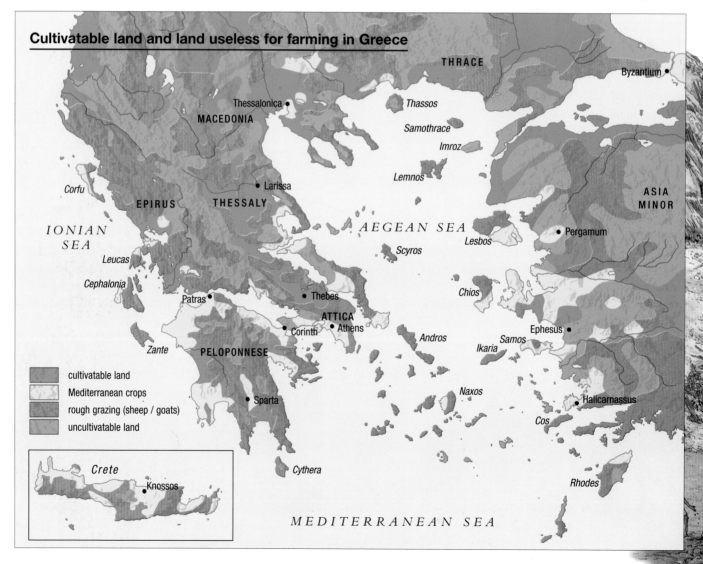

Cultivatable land and land useless for farming in Greece

THRACE
Byzantium

Thassos

Thessalonica
MACEDONIA
Samothrace

Imroz

Lemnos

Corfu
Larissa
ASIA MINOR

EPIRUS   THESSALY

IONIAN SEA
AEGEAN SEA
Pergamum

Scyros
Lesbos

Leucas

Cephalonia
Chios

Patras
Thebes

ATTICA
Ephesus
Corinth   Athens
Samos
Zante
Andros
Ikaria
PELOPONNESE

Sparta
Naxos
Halicarnassus

Cos

cultivatable land
Mediterranean crops
rough grazing (sheep / goats)
uncultivatable land

Crete
Cythera
Rhodes
Knossos

MEDITERRANEAN SEA

A farmer's hard lot

Only citizens of a *polis* (city-state, or citizen-state) may own land, but being a citizen and land-owner does not necessarily make a person rich. Greece is full of smallholders, who can barely make a living from their land. In the countryside of Attica most of the poorer farmers produce wheat and barley, while the wealthy and nobility own estates that produce wine and olive oil.

Although wheat is important, wheat-farming is not well managed. The farmers do not have enough land to practice crop rotation (moving crops between fields each season), so the soil's fertility gradually reduces. If crop production falls, it is the poor farmer who suffers because the wealthy Greeks can simply import what they need. This also pushes down the price the local farmer can get for his produce, and so he has to borrow money and get into debt—usually to a richer person, who then takes land as payment.

Sometimes, in order to pay off debts, the average farmer is forced to sell his children, wife, and even himself into a limited form of slavery. Situations like this explain why, from time to time, the rural people explode into rebellion against the city-dwellers who have claimed all the wealth.

Important farm animals

Wealthier farmers—especially the nobility who live in the big cities—employ poor citizens as managers and use slaves to farm their land. The young are often employed as herders to look after the goats and sheep that graze on the upper pastureland.

Given the rocky nature of the land, goats are the most important animals, since they can cope easily on the almost barren hilltops. The lack of suitable grazing means that cows are rare, and horses even more so, affordable only by the rich.

Below: A typical Greek farm. They are usually quite small, and only produce enough food to support a single family.

1. The best soil, close to the farm buildings, is reserved for raising fruits and vegetables.

2. Wheat and barley are the main crops, and this farm is lucky to have sufficient land for a sizeable wheat field.

3. Goats and sheep can graze on the scrubby grass of the lower hillsides.

4. Grapes are also grown on lower hillsides that face the south.

5. The higher ground, with its poor soil— useless for any other crops—is planted with olive trees.

The Farming Year

Greece is a land of farmers, and for those with a surplus of produce to sell the *agora*, or marketplace, is the center of their world.

The *agora* is the heart of every Greek city or town of reasonable size (*see page 64*). Early morning is a time of frantic bustle, as the farmers set up stalls of olive oil, pork, cheese, grain, fruit, eggs, and animal hides. Once they have sold their produce, the country people return to their farms, smallholders on foot, the better off riding the empty cart pulled by one of their oxen.

Selling is only a tiny part of the farmer's life—growing crops in poor soil is the more difficult part. The Greeks do not practice crop rotation. They sow crops one year and leave the field to lie fallow for the next to give the soil time to recover. This puts even more pressure on the scarce cultivable land.

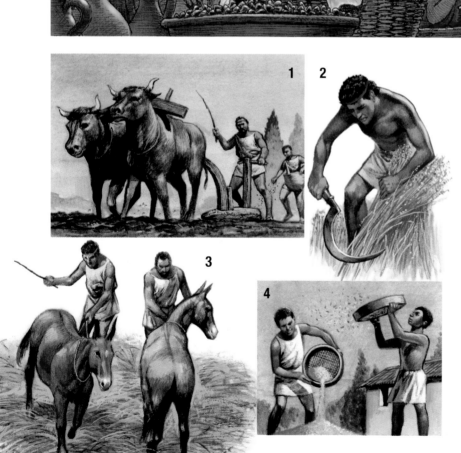

The grain harvest

Grain sown in October grows during the wettest months of the year. Oxen pull the plow, steered by one man, while another follows, scattering the seed by hand (**1**). Depending on the amount of winter rainfall, grain is harvested between May and July using sickles (**2**).

It is then threshed from the stalks in a manner similar to that employed by Egyptians, by driving mules over it on a circular stone threshing floor (**3**). Many of the early religious sanctuaries grew up around a threshing floor (*see map of Delphi, page 23, and also pages 90–93*).

The threshing process also removes the chaff, or outer husk of the grain kernels, and so threshing floors are often positioned in a place where the wind helps to blow the lighter chaff away. Otherwise, the young boys of the family winnow it by throwing the grain into the air on sieves (**4**).

Livestock

While horses are rare—except in Thessaly, where there is lots of pasture—most farmers keep oxen, donkeys, and mules as draft animals. Sheep and goats provide wool, hides, meat, and milk, which is also used to make cheese. Pigs are kept close to the farmhouse, where they can be watched to prevent them from scavenging in the vegetable patch, and in winter they provide extra heat once penned inside the house. Poultry is also valuable for both meat and eggs, but ducks and chickens have to be closely guarded from foxes, which are everywhere.

Farming wealth—vines and olives

Hill farmers keep bees and produce the honey that is the Greeks' main sweetener. Peas, lentils, beans, garlic, onions, and cabbage are plentiful, but the major source of agricultural wealth comes from cultivating olive trees and vines.

The vineyard owner needs the money he makes, because it takes a lot of workers to cultivate and harvest the vines—and slaves are not so numerous in rural Greece as in other countries (except around Athens, where they outnumber the citizen population). The vines are grown on terraced hillsides to get the best of the sun. Once ripened, the grapes are picked in September. They are then trodden underfoot in large vats made of wood or mortar, which slope down to an outlet.

After harvesting the grapes, men pulp the fruit underfoot in large vats to make wine.

Below: Picking olives by shaking the fruit loose and squeezing out the oil in a press.

The juice is collected in clay jars and left to ferment for about six months in a cool cellar. When the fermentation process has stopped, the wine is poured into large clay vessels called *amphorae* for ease of transport (*see page 68*).

Olive trees take about 16 years before they begin to yield usable fruit. Once again, only a wealthy farmer can afford this kind of investment, but the returns are huge. Olives are gathered by shaking the branches and collecting the fallen fruit in baskets. The fruit is pulped in a hand mill before the oil is extracted in a stone press.

Olive oil is used for cooking, lighting, washing, and in many beauty products; athletes rub themselves down with it. Greek oil is prized all around the Mediterranean.

The Colonies—in Search of Farming Land

Fertile land is in short supply in mountainous Greece, and land hunger drives many Greeks overseas to establish colonies. Before long, many of these emigrant farmer-communities have grown into major city-states in their own right.

In theory, a Greek colony is the property of its mother city, or *metropolis*. But in most cases the colonies are allowed to act independently. The creation of a new colony is a highly organized process. The settlement is set up as a mirror image of its *metropolis*, with the same political structure, laws, and even religious temples or cults as the parent city.

Colonies are almost always established on a coast for ease of communication by sea with the *metropolis*, and in areas where trading links have already been established. Greek colonies now exist all over the Aegean and Mediterranean Seas and on the shores of the Black Sea. The principal areas of

settlement beyond the Aegean are in Libya, southern Italy, Sicily, and even the coast of southern France.

All these regions produce goods that can be exported to Greece: wool from North Africa, Italy, and Asia Minor; grain from the Black Sea coast and the Crimea; grain, dye, and hides from Sicily; and cereals and papyrus from Egypt.

Right: Pythagoras of Crotone (569–500 BCE) is a mathematician and thinker, best known for his geometric theorem.

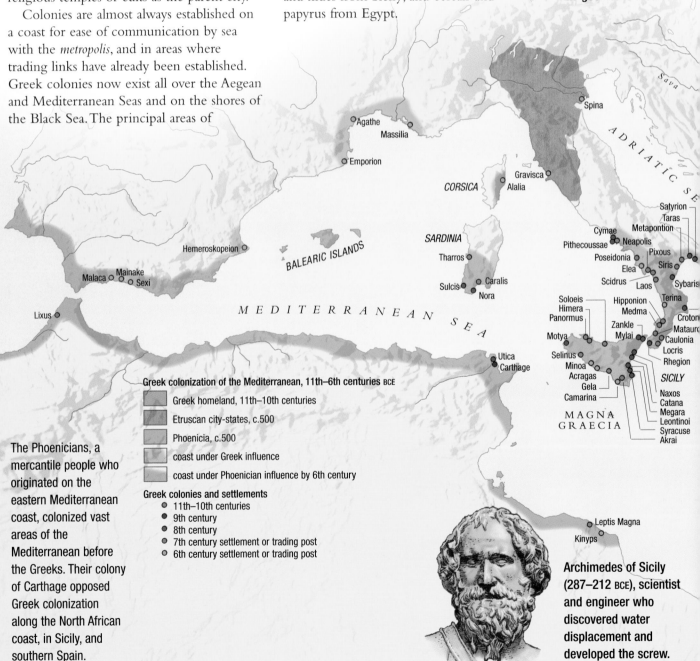

Greek colonization of the Mediterranean, 11th–6th centuries BCE

- Greek homeland, 11th–10th centuries
- Etruscan city-states, c.500
- Phoenicia, c.500
- coast under Greek influence
- coast under Phoenician influence by 6th century

Greek colonies and settlements
- 11th–10th centuries
- 9th century
- 8th century
- 7th century settlement or trading post
- 6th century settlement or trading post

The Phoenicians, a mercantile people who originated on the eastern Mediterranean coast, colonized vast areas of the Mediterranean before the Greeks. Their colony of Carthage opposed Greek colonization along the North African coast, in Sicily, and southern Spain.

Archimedes of Sicily (287–212 BCE), scientist and engineer who discovered water displacement and developed the screw.

So dense is the level of colonization in southern Italy and Greece, that the region has become known to the Romans as Magna Graecia (Greater Greece). Astonishing as it may seem, a handful of Greek cities has spawned hundreds of colonies clustered around the Mediterranean—as Socrates puts it, "like frogs around a pond."

Colonial history

The first colonies were set up in the 8th century in southern Italy and Sicily. The city-states of Athens and Sparta were most busy in developing colonies here, but the Corinthian colony of Syracuse is the most prosperous Sicilian settlement, closely followed by Acragas. In the early 7th century, colonies were founded around the Black Sea and the Hellespont strait (Dardanelles), most established by the island city-state of Miletos. The Libyan colony of Cyrene spawned further colonies of its own on the North African coast. The Ionian Greek settlement established at Massilia (Marseilles) in about 600 BCE has expanded into a thriving port that dominates trade between Greece and the French countryside.

The Greek colonies have produced some of the finest minds of the time; a handful of the most famous are shown on these pages.

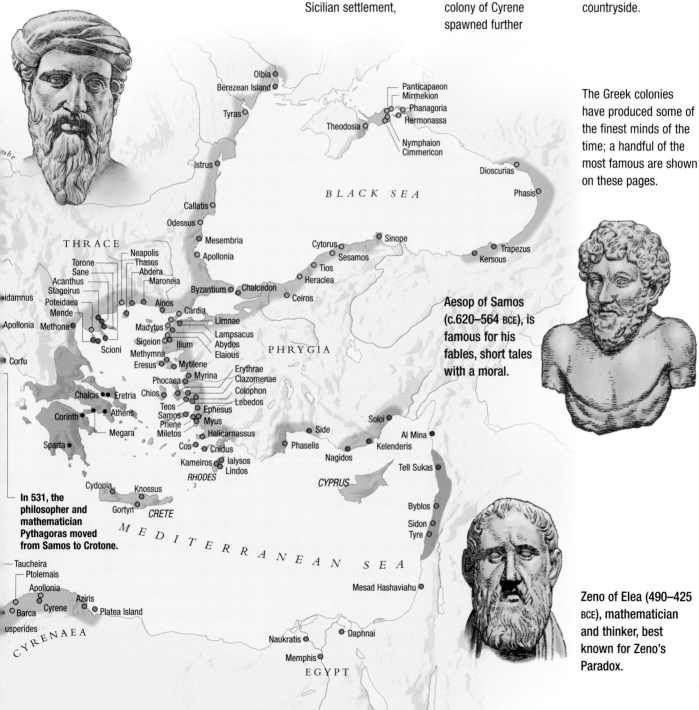

Aesop of Samos (c.620–564 BCE), is famous for his fables, short tales with a moral.

In 531, the philosopher and mathematician Pythagoras moved from Samos to Crotone.

Zeno of Elea (490–425 BCE), mathematician and thinker, best known for Zeno's Paradox.

35

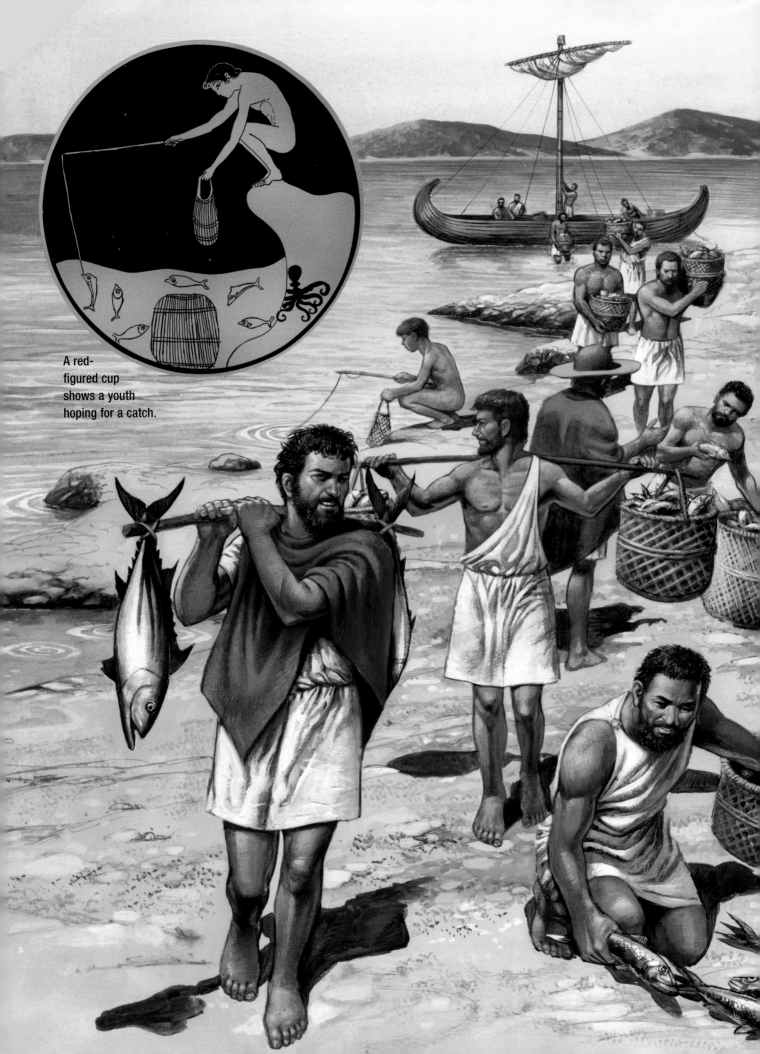

A red-
figured cup
shows a youth
hoping for a catch.

The Abundant Sea

With such a long coastline and so many islands, it comes as no surprise that fish is a popular item in the Greek diet, especially for the poorer classes.

Fishermen on the Gulf of Corinth

A fishing boat has just pulled into shore to unload a catch. One man has already arrived to start bargaining before the fish reach the *agora*, hoping to get the best for his family.

A young boy fishes with a line and hook, holding a landing basket in one hand. He has set a larger basket in the water to hold the caught fish, which keeps them fresh until he gets them home.

In the foreground, a fish-seller carries a basket laden with herring toward the *agora*. A pair of tunny fish are secured to the carrying pole over his friend's shoulders.

The ringing of the "fish bell" to announce the arrival of a fresh catch is the signal for a rush of householders to the *agora*. Such is the eagerness for fish that a tale is told about a recital by a lyre player whose entire audience dashed off when they heard the fish bell ring, with the exception of one deaf man. When the musician thanked him for staying to listen to the end of his playing, the old man looked up in horror and said, "What! Did I miss the fish bell?" and rushed off as fast as he could.

The catch

Fish are even more important to the numerous island-dwellers of the Aegean Sea. Few of these rocky outcrops are capable of raising substantial crops, and most foodstuffs have to be imported at great expense from the mainland, while the readily available seafood is cheap.

Large quantities of sardines are caught in Phaleron Bay at Piraeus. As the least expensive fish, sardines form a large part of the poorer classes' diet. For the better off, tunny is also plentiful, but the most prized are the great eels that are brought from Lake Kopaïs in Boeotia. Salted and smoked fish are brought in from the Black Sea ports and the colonies of the Spanish coast.

Fact box

The modern Greek word for "fish," *psari*, is derived from the ancient Greek word *opsarion*, meaning "delicacy."

Life has not changed much in 2500 years—this modern Greek fisherman attracts fish using an electrically powered light in place of the flaming torch the ancients would use.

Fishing is a serious business

The Greeks mainly use nets for fishing, but they also angle with hooks and lines. Squid and octopuses are caught by spearing them with tridents, usually at night by the light of torches.

Small sailing boats, crewed by up to ten men, go out at night and fish with nets and torches that attract the fish. The boats are usually owned by a single family, and the crewmen are paid for their work either in cash from the eventual sale, or in kind by a share of the catch. Sometimes a cooperative owns a boat between several poorer fishermen. No one regards fishing as a recreational activity; it is always a serious business and, besides, the proper sport for young aristocrats is hunting.

Putting Food on the Table

For the average Greek, the main diet is simple, and largely free of meat because of its expense. But dining in a wealthier home provides a huge variety of appetizing dishes.

Two men lounge outside a civic bakery and chat as they wait for their loaves of bread to finish baking. A boy brings a bag of grain to hand over to get bread made for his family.

Bread plays a very important role in every-day life. Common breads for ordinary meals are made by kneading flour with water, or with water and honey, sometimes with oil or honey and wine (*oinomelo*). The breads vary in the manner of baking as well as in shape, and whether they are "raised" by using grape yeast or left unleavened.

By adding fresh or dried fruit, cheese and herbs, or olives, many different luxury breads are made, especially for festivals and holidays. The Greeks have more than 50 kinds of bread. In the cities, public bakeries and ovens are built by the government for everyone's use and they have become popular places for men to visit the neighbors and discuss the state of affairs.

Three meals a day

Most food is produced in the region around the *polis*, although maritime cities like Athens also import luxury goods and foreign delicacies. Typically, Greeks eat three meals a day, in the early morning, at midday, and in the evening. Breakfast is normally a light meal—bread dipped in wine or a lump of cheese is common at all levels of society. Lunch is a little more substantial, often including olives, figs, cheese, bread, and wine. The main meal of the day is dinner, usually a barley porridge accompanied by fresh and cooked vegetables.

Among the wealthy, dinner often involves inviting male friends home for a meal, or even eating at a "dining club" (equivalent of a restaurant). The evening meal is eaten while reclining on an *anaklintra* (couch), and slaves bring food, wine, and finger bowls to the diners. The women of the household are excluded from these formal dinners, except as slaves or as *hetairai* (*see page 43*).

Meat for the table

Although sheep, pigs, goats, and some cattle are raised for the table, meat is a luxury. At home, a family is more than happy to have the occasional sausage or perhaps a locally trapped hare. Pheasants and chickens are available to boost at least one meal a week, and cheese made from the milk of sheep and goats is produced in great volume.

Fish, shellfish, squid, and eels are consumed in many different ways: fried, baked, stewed, dried, and smoked. Richer families may extend their diet to caviar, oysters, and turtles.

Preserving for the winter

Fruit and vegetables are readily available fresh during the summer. Fruits are eaten in all possible manners, while vegetables—if not cooked in a stew—are preferred raw with an olive oil dressing. In the late summer, it is necessary to preserve fruit and vegetables for the winter. Fruit is preserved by sun-drying and then packing it in clay jars, or by placing fruits in honey, carefully ensuring that no one fruit touches another. Green vegetables are preserved simply, by putting them in a vessel treated with pitch.

In a wealthy home, any meat—such as wild game, freshly caught fish, and pork—is hung in the chimney, where the fires of the kitchen "smoke" and preserve it for later consumption (*see illustration on pages 52–53, point 6*).

Seasonings and flavorings

The Greeks love to combine sweet and sour flavors, the basic ones being honey, vinegar, and *garos* (a sauce based on fermented salted fish). Many herbs and spices are also used—mustard, coriander (cilantro), cumin, oregano, dill, parsley, mint, pine nuts, poppy seeds, sesame, fennel, and aniseed are among the most popular seasonings. And few Greek meals remain unflavored by garlic and onions.

The Greek general and historian Xenophon amusingly remembers how the guests at a dinner laughed at the newly-wed young man who refused his portion of onions in order to keep his breath sweet for his bride.

This newly-wed loves onions, but fears his dear bride will not.

A collection of everyday eating bowls, utensils, and food from the late 5th century.

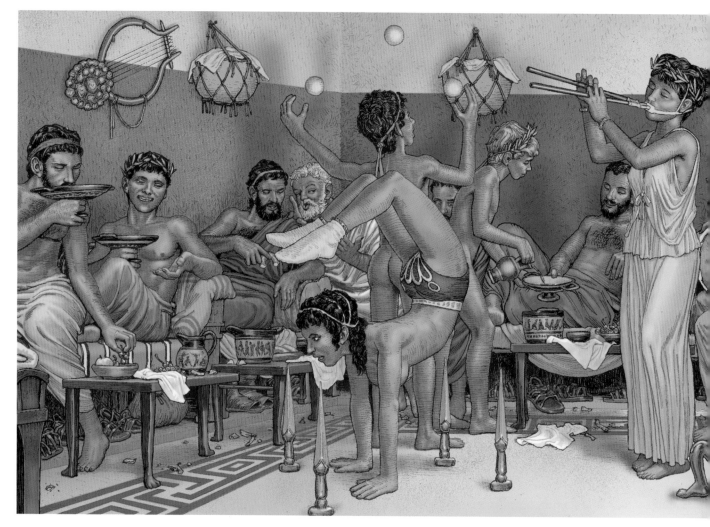

Wine and the Symposium

Wine is the common drink of poor and rich alike, but wines vary in quality and therefore in price. Among the wealthy, drinking wine is an important part of the evening banquet.

A *symposium* in its final stage: as the guests nibble sweets, more wine is served, and entertainers take to the floor to bring the night's meal to a merry close.

The *symposium* (a feast or formal meal) of wealthy men—usually held at home—is typically Greek. Eating and drinking is a social activity, an opportunity to meet others and discuss politics, listen to music, play games, and enjoy companionship. A *symposium* often lasts from the early afternoon until late at night.

Men are the only guests, because—apart from eating and drinking—the important part of a *symposium* is the conversation about philosophical, artistic, and political matters. These are mental exercises fit for men, but not for women, who the Greeks believe cannot understand these subjects properly.

As the guests lie down on their *anaklintra*

(couch), slaves serve *oinomelo*, wine mixed with honey, and bread. The dishes then follow in a strict order. First come several appetizers and fruit, then fresh fish and meat prepared in several interesting ways.

The *symposium*'s second phase is called the *epidorpion*, which means dessert, but it is much more than a selection of sweets. Several kinds of pies, sweets, dried fruits, nuts, and cheeses are brought in.

A popular sweet is *baklava*, the baked confection of nuts and honey between layers of thin bread dough that Greek mercenary soldiers brought back from Assyria centuries before. Along with these delights comes the most important item—more wine.

Mixing wine and water

The host decides how much water should be mixed with the wine. Wine, stored in an *amphora* vessel, is strained through fine cloth to catch sediment deposited from the fermentation process, to be mixed with water in a large vessel called a *krater*. The mixture is then transferred from the *krater* to a jug called an *oinchoe* for pouring into cups.

In general, the dilution starts with several parts of water to one part of wine, but as the evening progresses the wine begins to dominate, until the guests are drinking their wine undiluted.

The host is responsible for getting his guests drunk, but not before they have enjoyed debate and argument, and recited poetry. As they become less capable of speech, the entertainment begins—professional dancers, musicians, even acrobat performances.

With the *symposium* concluded, the host can retire to his bedchamber, while his guests stumble to their homes, their way lit by slaves bearing torches.

The importance of wine

The success of a *symposium* reflects on the status and wealth of the host, never more so than in the quality of his wine. The best wines come from the Aegean islands, especially Lesbos and Chios. Wine is available in the three basic types—white, red, and "black" (a very deep-bodied red wine).

It is categorized as being sweet, the honeyed, the ripe, and the soft. The very expensive black wines are so heavy that is only sensible to dilute them with water—at least at the start of a *symposium*!

To the Greeks, wine-drinking is more than an enjoyment, it also has religious symbolism—it is the only drink able to soothe even the quarrelsome gods of Olympus. Dionysus, god of fertility, wine, and theater, is honored at the time of the grape harvest and when the first new wines are ready to drink in February.

This, the most important Dionysian festival, is called the Anthesteria and it celebrates the god through processions and wine-drinking contests (*see also page* 47) in what is effectively a week-long *symposium*— but with the difference that women may attend the festivities.

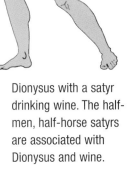

Dionysus with a satyr drinking wine. The half-men, half-horse satyrs are associated with Dionysus and wine.

The Victorian painter Lawrence Alma-Tadema painted a Dionysian festival scene (**below**). Behind the female dancers, a celebrant has slumped under the influence of the wine.

CHAPTER 3

The Greeks at Home and Work

The Family—the Role of Women

Greek women are more subordinate to men than even those in Mesopotamia or Egypt. From the poorest to the richest homes, women are considered the property of their father, and later of their husband, and are treated accordingly.

With the exception of Sparta (*see "The Spartan difference"*), Greek women have very limited freedom outside the home, and have no legal and few social rights. The *kyrios* or head of the household (the father, husband, or other male relative) legally owns all the women under his roof, an ownership that passes from father to husband when a daughter marries.

Women have no right to vote or to legal help, and with few exceptions they may not own or inherit property. The role of a wife is to run the household, bear children and take care of them, manage slaves and servants, and attend to her husband's needs.

Stuck at home

She is a virtual prisoner within her home and rarely leaves it, except during certain religious festivals, such as the Panathenaic Procession and the festivals of Dionysus. Other special occasions are few, beyond attending weddings and funerals, and visiting female neighbors for brief periods.

Wives of poorer citizens may be more fortunate than those who are better off, since they sometimes have to work outside of the home as servants or craftspeople. On the other hand, in a family with few or no slaves, the poor housewife has to do almost everything, whereas women do not do the housework in a wealthier home.

The housewife's day

Female slaves look after the cooking, cleaning, and work in the fields. A male slave watches the door, to make sure no one comes in when the husband is away, and another acts as a *paedogogus* (tutor) to the young male children.

Women do not even go out to do the shopping. It is the task of men to leave for

the *agora* in the morning to shop for daily requirements such as fish, cheese, olives, and vegetables, and occasional luxuries such as trinket boxes and jewelry.

A woman's day is mostly spent in her quarters, called the *gynaeceum*, spinning yarn and weaving. She makes all the clothes for the family and the slaves, hangings to brighten the walls and cover the windows, bed blankets and cushions. Fortunately, this is not viewed as being a boring job, but is considered a noble task, even for aristocratic wives and daughters.

Young girls are expected to spend their day with their mothers, learning how to run the home and to spin and weave, ready for the time when they get married.

The *hetaira*

Among men, the word *hetairos* means a male companion, and the use of the word in a feminine form—*hetaira*—implies that female companions are expected to be trained and sociable in a way that wives are not. *Hetairai* are professional courtesans who entertain the male guests at a *symposium*.

They are expected to be good at reciting poetry, playing music, and dancing. Most importantly, they must be capable of holding an intelligent conversation among men—which means discussing politics, philosophy, and the arts.

This is how Greek men divide women. A *hetaira* is almost an honorary male, a companion almost as good as a man but blessed with female beauty, whereas wives and daughters are essentially property.

Apart from their maternal qualifications to run a household, being intelligent is considered unnecessary for female relatives, any more than it is for a slave. Even the celebrated philosopher Aristotle writes that the ability to think is not found in slaves, nor in women.

Upper left: Married women and daughters spend their time in the *gynaeceum*, weaving and making the family's clothes.

The right of life and death

The head of the family has complete control over the household, including grandparents, unmarried sisters, widowed aunts, and any orphans. His wife has no legal rights, even over her children. If the family cannot afford to feed another mouth, or a child is sickly or deformed, the father can decide to leave a newborn infant on a remote mountainside to die.

With this level of power, it is not surprising that women are considered untouchable by any other than their husbands. But it is not so for the men, or for the one type of female who might be considered to be free, the *hetaira*.

Left: On the rare occasions when a married woman goes out, she is accompanied by a slave for her protection, and perhaps another to fetch and carry.

Right: A regretful father tears a baby from its weeping mother to expose the child in a remote place.

The Spartan difference

The role of women in warlike Sparta is quite different from other parts of Greece. There, women can own property—in fact more than a third of Spartan land is owned by women—and daughters are allowed to inherit as well as sons. Spartan women are given a good education in both the arts and athletics (something no other Greek city would allow), and often hold real political power within the *polis*.

The reasons for this difference can be explained by Sparta's warrior-nation character. The nation, not the family, is the center of life for every man. Boys leave home to begin their military training at the age of seven and because, as husbands, men are rarely at home and take no part in child-rearing, Spartan women are free to take charge of almost everything outside of the army.

Marriage and Divorce

For most Greeks, being in love is not a reason for getting married. There are far more important motives for a wedding than romance.

While married women rarely leave their home, young girls are hardly ever let out of its female quarters—they should remain unseen even by male members of their own family. (This is in sharp contrast to Sparta, where young girls train openly at sports with the young men.)

Girls are considered to have reached marriageable age at puberty, and certainly before 16. Given her housebound seclusion there can be no question of courtship with a prospective husband, and most couples never even meet until the wedding day. When the head of the household (*kyrios*) decides a daughter is ready to be married, he chooses a husband for her and negotiates with the prospective bridegroom's family.

The happy outcome of this is the *gamos* or marriage, which happens in two parts, first being the *engeyesis* or engagement ceremony. Again, there is no romance involved—this is a thorough and legally binding verbal contract between the two families which does not concern the girl. The *engeyesis* is pledged by the future husband and the girl's father clasping hands. The agreement includes settling a dowry (a gift from the bride's family); all oaths are sworn in front of witnesses.

A man is usually about 30 when he decides to marry, so he is perfectly capable of making up his own mind as to whom he should marry—or more to the point, to which family he should ally himself. He may well consult his father about this; fathers often arrange marriages for their sons in order to strengthen the family position. Status and self-interest are the main motives.

Purifying bride and groom

The second part—*ekdosis*, the marriage ceremony—involves giving away the bride to the groom. This begins on the evening the bride moves to her new home and consists of three important preparations. First a sacrifice is made to the gods and goddesses

Ritual bathing of the bride and groom

who protect the marriage-bed—Zeus, Hera, Artemis, and Apollo. The sacrificial offering usually consists of all the bride's toys and any objects associated with her childhood.

Next, a torchlit procession is led to a special fountain known as a *callirhoe* to bring back water in a long-necked vase called a *loutrophoros* for the ritual sacred bath.

In his own home, the bridegroom also ritually bathes in sacred water taken from the fountain.

The wedding day

On the wedding day both houses are decorated with garlands of olive and laurel. After a sacrifice in the bride's house, she is taken to the place of the wedding feast accompanied by her sisters, girlfriends, and her *nympheutria* or maid of honor. From the other direction comes the bridegroom with his *parochos* or best man.

Men and women are seated apart at the banquet, which includes sesame cakes—a symbol of fertility. After eating, the

Divorce for men

A man can always divorce his wife—even if there is no real reason. But he is forced by law to divorce her if she is caught committing adultery, otherwise he is liable to *iatimia*—the loss of his rights as a citizen. There is one check against an easy divorce: a husband who returns his wife back to her family home also has to return her dowry.

Greek men marry to have children, so failure to bear any is a common reason for a man to divorce his wife. Daughters can marry into other families, thus forming alliances, but sons are needed to continue a father's line and to bury him with full rites. There must be at least one son to guarantee the cult honors which he, the father, performed for his ancestors, and which are essential for the well-being of the dead.

Divorce for women

It is much harder for a woman to divorce a husband, since she is presumed incapable of managing her own affairs. She can appeal in writing to the *archon* (minister) responsible for justice, but her husband's unfaithfulness is not considered a reason for divorce because Greek society accepts complete freedom for men. If she can prove violence against her or ill-treatment the *archon* may consent, but she faces many problems.

A wife divorced by her husband may return to her family home with little disgrace, but everyone frowns on a woman who divorces her husband. Shunned by neighbors and even by family, there is little future for her. Many such women are then forced to become another man's mistress or a *hetaira* (see page 43).

guests offer their presents to the bride, and then she is taken to her new home, riding in a wagon pulled by mules or oxen. With her she carries a sieve and a cooking gridiron—symbols of her domestic role.

Relatives and friends follow on foot, carrying torches to the music of flutes and lyres. At the groom's house, the couple are showered with nuts and dried figs, and offered a wedding cake made with sesame and honey before they retire to the *thalamos* or bridal chamber. Outside, the wedding guests sing wedding songs as loudly as possible to scare away evil spirits.

Leading a happy wedding procession, the new couple reach the groom's house.

Below: A man can divorce his wife and send her back to her own family, while keeping their children with him. She may never see them again.

Left: In Athens it is a custom for a young boy—whose parents must still be alive—to go about with a basket of cakes and say, "I fled from misfortune, I found a better lot." This symbolizes the sensible move the groom is making in marrying and starting his own family.

Birth and Children

Although a daughter may be desirable and a son essential, the Greeks do not have large families because of poverty or to avoid estates being divided among too many male heirs.

A grandmother prepares to feed her daughter's hungry baby, which cries for attention and shakes its rattle. The child's high chair acts as a potty too. Mother is busy chatting with a visiting friend.

To avoid having too many children, abortion and exposure of newborn infants are practiced. Abortion is legal, since the law considers the unborn child to be its father's property. A mother, however, needs her husband's consent for an abortion, and a slave girl that her of her owner.

Infanticide is also allowed as long as the child has not been named or accepted as a member of society. The father does not kill the child but abandons it—so weather, starvation, or wild animals are responsible for the death. Not all exposed children die— sympathetic foster parents rescue some, others are enslaved. The rescued baby is a common theme in Greek mythology, the most famous being that of King Oedipus, who later returned home to unknowingly kill his real father and marry his mother.

In harsh Sparta, newborn children are presented to the elders and tested by immersion in ice-cold water. Those who fail through being weak or sickly are exposed on Mount Taygetos in order to protect the strength of the race.

Childbirth

Children are born at home, with all the women of the household crowding around the mother. The most experienced in birthing helps with the delivery, but if there is a problem a doctor or a midwife can be summoned.

The world at large is informed of a birth by the family hanging something over the front door—an olive branch for a boy, a strip of woolen material for a girl. A week after the birth, a family festival known as the *amphidromia* is held, a purification ceremony for the mother and all those who helped during her labor.

The ritual also admits the baby as a member of its social group. From now on, the child is an accepted member of the community and the father no longer has the right to end its life.

The baby is named on the tenth day after its birth, with the family members all assembled for another sacrifice and a banquet. The relatives bring gifts for the baby, in particular amulets for good luck.

Above: A goose and rider and a jointed doll are just some of the toys to amuse children.

Right: A boy plays with a hoop on a red-figured cup decoration.

Festivals and the *phratria*

Two important festivals mark the early life of a boy when he is about three years old, the Anthesteria and the Apatouria. The first is a festival dedicated to Dionysus, and young boys, crowned with flowers, are encouraged to compete in the festival's second-day event known as Wine Jugs.

In this, the competitors are given a measure of diluted wine in a special jug. At a command, everyone empties their jugs, and the first to finish drinking is the winner. Adults taking part must drink almost half a gallon, so it is as well that children are given much smaller jugs!

The Apatouria is a gathering of the father's *phratria* (clan or family association) in October, when the boy is introduced. The Apatouria is a time to catch up on news, make sacrifices, and register new members of the family. The father swears that his son is born to him of a citizen-mother, which establishes the boy's rights to citizenship later.

Toys and games

Greeks love to give their children presents of toys, which they can buy from sellers in the marketplace (*agora*). Some toys are made at home by the children themselves—houses, wagons, and ships out of strips of leather. In a larger courtyard, or outside in the farmyard, there may be swings, and boys play with kites, hoops, model carts, whipping tops, and wheels pulled along with poles.

While babies have rattles made from hollow containers with pebbles inside to entertain them, older boys play team games with balls made of pigs' bladders, whipped along with sticks. Games of leapfrog, piggyback, and blindman's buff are all enjoyed. But playtime comes to an end when a boy reaches the age of seven, and it is time for school to begin.

A Boy's Education

It is a father's civic duty to provide for his son's education. After a care-free early childhood, boys are schooled to become model citizens—statesmen or soldiers—while girls are prepared for marriage.

Above: Fragments of a red-figured vase show a school at work. To the left, one youth practices music. In the center, a teacher holds up an alphabet chart for another boy to read out, under the stern eye of his *paedogogus*.

Left: A boy practices writing with a stylus on a three-leaf wax tablet.

Below: From the age of 12, physical education becomes an important part of schooling.

Only a son can continue the family line. As for his sister, once a girl is married her future happiness is the responsibility of her new husband and she is unlikely to see her father again. As a result it is only the boys who get a proper schooling.

Pupils living in cities are taught to become productive members of their democratic society. Because all male citizens are expected to take an active part in debates, justice, and local or city government, they must be fluent in reading, writing, and basic arithmetic. In country regions the level of education is lower than in the cities.

Vocational training

Since most states imitate Athens' institutions and social organization, it is best to see how education of boys is handled there. Athens has no state-run education system, so families unable to afford the cost of private schooling apprentice their sons to a master craftsman or a merchant.

The apprenticeship system encourages youngsters to improve their education while learning a useful trade. Apprenticeships, of at least six years, are usually begun at 12 years of age for such occupations as builder, merchant, potter, carpenter, or shipwright.

Privileged school network

For the sons of wealthier citizens, the options are far more appealing. When he is about seven, the boy is removed from his nurse and given to the care of a *paedogogus*, a selected household slave who accompanies him everywhere and is permitted to punish the boy if he behaves badly.

The *paedogogus* takes the boy to school and stays with him to ensure he pays attention to his lessons and works hard. Classes are held in teachers' private homes. Since music is such an important part of life in Greece, boys are also taught to sing and play the lyre and flute.

There is a law that forbids children to be on the streets in the hours of darkness, so classes take place from about half an hour after sunrise until half an hour before sunset. This makes for a particularly long day in the summer, but a mercifully short one in winter.

A girl's education stops at the point her brother starts school. Slave girls may teach the finer points of manners and the skills required to run a household, while her mother teaches the arts of spinning and weaving cloth.

Hurrying home before it grows dark, boys and their *paedogogi* leave school.

From school to *gymnasium*

When he comes of age, every male Greek citizen is expected to be a soldier at some level, from *hoplite* (infantryman) to *strategos* (general)—the army is the route to the highest political positions. Therefore, physical fitness is considered every bit as important as academic learning, if not more so.

Once a boy reaches the age of 12, his education expands to include physical training, which now takes precedence over any other subject. The relative calm of the private teacher's home is replaced by the noise and activity of the local *gymnasium*. It gets its name from the Greek word *gymnos*, meaning "naked," for at this school the boys undergo their physical exercises without any clothing as they learn to compete with each other and how to cooperate in teams.

Education in Sparta

Like his Athenian counterpart, a Spartan boy is taken from his family at the age of seven. However, his education is completely different. He is raised in a dormitory class, where his group learns the skills needed to become first-class soldiers.

Conditions are literally *spartan*. Clothing is minimal even in the harshest winter, punishments severe, and academic tuition almost non-existent. Spartans are trained to accept tough campaign conditions without complaining. Food is strictly rationed as a part of this hardship training. The youths are often hungry enough to steal. If caught, the child is punished severely—not for stealing, but for being caught in the act.

At 12, boys are introduced to military training, which continues until the trainee reaches 20 years of age. Most youths are accepted into the army, while those that fail to make the grade serve in military administration and form a pool of reservists.

There is no other option than a life in the army for a Spartan man, until he is either too old to serve or dies in battle— whichever is the sooner.

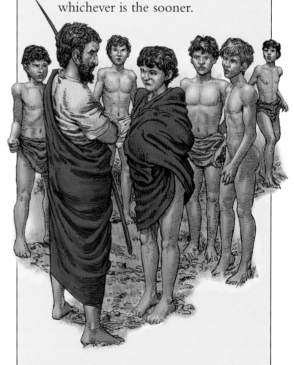

A hungry boy stole a fox and hid it under his cloak. But the fox began biting him. Rather than be caught out, the boy gritted his teeth and let the fox tear at his stomach until it killed him.

The Gymnasium and Military Training

Between the ages of 12 and 18, boys undergo rigorous physical training while still fitting in lessons between bouts of exercise. It is a system designed to create fit, healthy, and educated leaders of men.

All *gymnasia* are centered around an open-air sports ground called a *palaestra*—which takes its name from the principal exercise of *pale* (wrestling). A *paedotribes* teaches the boys gymnastics—with the aid of a long stick when necessary. They limber up to music, then compete in sports such as wrestling, running, and discus- and javelin-throwing. With exercises concluded, the class retires to a bathhouse to clean up.

Academic lessons take place in the cool of the covered arcade, or colonnade, that surrounds the *palaestra*, with classes arranged by age, taking turns in lessons and physical training. In Athens the older youths might also attend an academy for tutoring in the finer disciplines, such as appreciation and participation in music, science, and the arts. Athens is a society that emphasizes cultural development.

Coming of age

Schooling lasts for about 12 years, ending at the age of 18, but boys are considered to have come of age at 16. On the third day of Apatouria, October's family gathering, a boy cuts his hair to show that his childhood is over. And once he has completed his last two years in the *gymnasium*, the young man is eligible for military training and special education in religious and political duties.

His first task as a man is to report to and register his name with his *deme* (local community) and prove his right to citizenship. Normally, this is a formality, since his father will have registered this right with his clan (*phratria*) when the boy was aged three (*see page 47*).

A healthy mind in a healthy body is the Greek ideal. In a busy *gymnasium*, one group of youths are put through their paces by the *paedotribes* on the *palaestra*, while teachers give academic lessons under the cool shade of a colonnade.

The oath of an *ephebos*

Youths between the ages of 18 and 20, known as *epheboi*, are subject to the rigors of army life. An *ephebos* spends two years of military service on the frontiers of Attica, the region surrounding Athens. He also plays an important part in some religious events, such as the Eleusinian Mysteries and the Panathenaic Festival. Along with the other newly conscripted recruits, he swears an oath, binding on him as a citizen:

- I will not disgrace these sacred arms.
- I will not desert my companions in battle.
- I will defend our sacred and public institutions.
- I will leave my fatherland better and greater, as far as I am able.
- I will obey the magistrates and the laws and defend them against those who seek to destroy them.

My witnesses are the gods… and the boundaries of the fatherland.

Becoming a full citizen

An *ephebos* may continue his academic education while he is under military instruction, if he wishes to. This is administered by sophists ("wise men") hired for the purpose. These roving tutors advise on the skills considered vital for civic advancement and statesmanship—oratory, persuasion, rhetoric, reasoning, philosophy, and logic.

Many sophists have set up their own institutes of higher learning, the most famous of which is the Academy run by Plato. The result is a breed of skilled young civic leaders, eager to further their political and military careers through the advancement of Athens. These leaders have helped shape all of Greece and share responsibility for its successes and failures.

At the age of 20 a youth is no longer an *ephebos*. He can attend the *ecclesia* (citizens' assembly) and begin his life as a citizen. However, while he remains fit and healthy he will continue to bear arms when the state requires it (*see page 80*).

An Athenian Merchant's Home

Most ancient Greeks' homes are small dwellings, but in the larger cities, such as Athens, wealthier merchants can afford more luxury. But even the homes of the rich are not very large by modern standards.

Unlike the Greeks' marvellous temples, ordinary houses are built of mud bricks. There are few windows to the outside, and the heart of the home is the courtyard. This open space may be large in farm-estate houses, but much smaller in town houses like the one illustrated here. The house usually has a single floor, with the reception rooms, slave quarters, kitchen, private rooms, and bedrooms surrounding the courtyard. Some city houses boast an upper floor for the family bedrooms.

Few homes have a bathroom. The men bathe at the *gymnasium*, while women wash in clay basins—bronze if the family can afford it—often mounted on a pedestal.

Wives are expected to spend their lives in isolation, permitted to run a household but rarely allowed to mingle with people outside the home. Even when the man of the house entertains, his guests will be other men, and they dine in a suite of rooms separate from the rest of his family.

1. The chimney is just a covered opening in the pantile roof.

2. In the *andron*, or dining room, the merchant's male guests recline on *anaklintrae* couches to dine. They are served by household slaves and entertained by a musician.

3. Anteroom to the *andron*. A slave brings food from the kitchen.

4. Storeroom, with a door to the street, for keeping grain, preserved dry goods, and fresh food.

5. Slaves cook food in the large kitchen. They are usually paid for their work and will be well treated.

6. The room next to the kitchen doubles as a chimney. The smoke is drawn through holes in the kitchen wall. Fish and meat are hung on its wall and become smoked, in order to preserve them for consumption in winter.

7. Porch. A janitor guards the front door.

8. Staircase to the upper floor gallery.

9. The *herm*. These statues are used to mark street corners and larger houses.

10. Courtyard open to the sky, with a small household shrine at its center. This is the heart of the Greek home, where the children play and the family spends the daylight hours. It has a covered veranda around all four sides.

11. Gallery on upper floor around the courtyard.

12. The wife in the *gynaeceum*, her private chamber, working at her loom. Wives and daughters make all the clothes, blankets, and wall coverings for the home.

13. Mud-brick walls built on a stone base. Floors are of mortar.

14. Greek houses only have a few, small windows to the exterior to keep the heat out in summer and retain heat from small braziers during winter. Most light is provided by the open courtyard.

Plan of the house

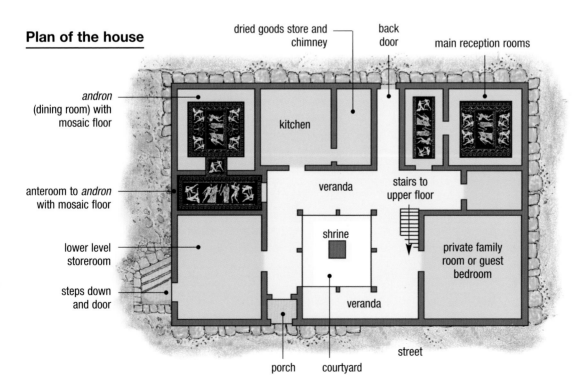

dried goods store and chimney

back door

main reception rooms

andron (dining room) with mosaic floor

kitchen

anteroom to *andron* with mosaic floor

veranda

stairs to upper floor

lower level storeroom

shrine

steps down and door

private family room or guest bedroom

veranda

porch   courtyard

street

1

6

5

2

3

4

8

10

7

11

12

14

13

9

Greeks call
a burglar
a "wall digger"
because in the
absence of
windows, he
simply burrows
through the flimsy
mud walls.

What the Greeks Wear

In a land where the climate is generally warm—frequently extremely hot—and in which the human body is considered a beautiful object, loose, flowing garments are desirable.

Woolen or flaxen tunics (*chiton*, seen far right), short for men, ankle-length for women, are the basic form of clothing. The tunic is complemented by a long, flowing *peplos* for women, sometimes covered by a cloak or *himation* (seen in red). Outdoors, women invariably cover their heads with a veil or the raised *himation*, but they are shown here uncovered so the clothes may be easily seen. Men may also sport a *himation* (brown) or the shorter *chlamys* (blue). Footwear ranges from light sandals to sturdy walking boots. Workmen (above) and laboring slaves usually wear only a loincloth.

All Greek clothing is essentially made from one or two large square pieces of cloth flung skillfully around the body and secured by a few well-placed pins. This costume is easily adjusted—it can be expanded into flowing draperies or contracted into an easy working dress by a few artful hitches.

The most common form of dress for both men and women is the *chiton*, a large rectangular tunic of wool or linen cloth, extending to the knee for men and the ankle for women.

Chiton and himation

With men the chiton's left side is left open, fastened by *fibulae*, elegantly wrought pins of silver, gold, or bone. In the closed side there is a slit for the arm. A girdle is usually worn about the waist, and, if one wishes, the skirt of the *chiton* may be pulled up through it, and allowed to hang down in front, giving the effect of a blouse.

The arms are left bare, as is the head,

although leather sandals, a hat, and a cloak called a *himation* provide extra protection from the elements when outdoors. *Epheboi* cadets and younger men often wear another shorter type of cloak called a *chlamys*, particularly when out hunting or riding.

A lack of tailors

Men working at a trade frequently wear a short skirt, belted at the waist, while a longer version extending from the waist to the ankles is sometimes worn in the evening at a feast (*symposium*). Male nudity is not considered scandalous, particularly when taking part in sporting events, at the baths, or in the home.

A man's simple woolen garments have usually been slowly and laboriously spun and woven by his wife and daughters, so they are hard-wearing and last for a long time. And fashions (at least in the cut of the garments) seldom change. A consequence of this is that there are very few Greek tailors, only cloth merchants, bleachers, and dyers.

The ladies' *peplos*

Women also wear a *peplos* over the *chiton*, a long flowing robe, tubular in shape, that ranges in design from the plain and simple to the highly decorated. A *peplos* is placed over the head and made to fit closely at the shoulder with fasteners and held at the waist with a girdle. The arms are left bare. The lower edge is often finished with a colored braid. The *peplos* is open at the right side and hangs in folds from the shoulder.

Saffron yellow is a very popular color, but clothes are also dyed violet, purple, or red. Very dark blue colors, such as indigo, indicate a person is in mourning.

While women take a bath at home, the men use the baths at the *gymnasium*.

Hairstyles

Once, men wore their hair long and sported long beards, but now a much shorter cut is popular, with a clean-shaven face or perhaps neatly trimmed facial hair for older men.

Women usually cover their hair when out of doors, either by pulling up the *himation* or wearing a veil. Their hair is worn long, and often dyed. Girls like to style theirs in a flowing manner or in ringlets, but married women usually wear their hair up, secured in place by ribbons, pins, headbands, or scarves.

Bracelets, rings, earrings, necklaces and cosmetics give more adornment. Eyes are darkened with mascara, the skin paled with lead powder and cheeks rouged. Creams and beauty lotions are popular.

However, the modest matron wears cosmetics with caution—an Athenian comedy play observes: "If you go out in summer, two streaks of black run from your eyes; perspiration makes a red furrow from your cheeks to your neck; and when your hair touches your face it is blanched with white lead."

A young woman inspects her hair in a polished bronze mirror, while a servant girl holds open a case with a necklace for her mistress. Beside her stands a *thymiaterion*, or incense burner, and on the low table are small *pyxides*, in which the cosmetics are kept.

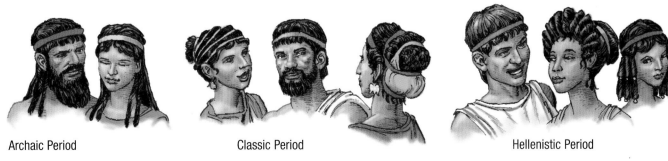

Archaic Period   Classic Period   Hellenistic Period

Crafts and Trades—Pottery

There may be few tailors about, but the Greeks have many other jobs to occupy them. The most widespread is the craft of pottery, which the Greeks have raised to a high art form.

A wealthy foreigner, a *metic*, shops for a gift in the display area of this Athenian pottery. The rear of the house is a hive of activity:

1. Most pots are made on a wheel, with an apprentice turning the wheel for the potter.

2. Large, complex pots are made in separate pieces and joined together. Handles are shaped by hand and joined on with wet slip clay later.

3. Once the finished pot has dried out, an artist decorates it.

Greek pottery is intended for everyday use, but as well as being functional it is usually beautifully decorated with paintings. These depict mythological scenes, famous heroes and their deeds, sporting events, and scenes of everyday life.

Skilled Greek potters are found in a city's *kerameikos*, or the pottery quarter. Their workshops are usually quite small, employing only five or six men. Here, they make large storage jars, cooking pots, lamps, roof tiles, and beautiful domestic ware such as vases, plates, bowls, jugs, wine cups, and *kraters* for mixing wine and water.

The more decorative pots are made by two people—the potter and the artist who paints it.

An *amphora* is a two-handled storage jar for wine, oil, and free-flowing commodities, such as grain.

A *hydria* is a jar for fetching water from public fountains. It has three handles; two short ones on the side for lifting, and a third—here facing directly out of the picture—for pouring.

Calyx krater

2

The decorated pots are fired (baked) in a beehive-shaped kiln. It has three openings: a loading door, a top air vent, and a furnace opening in which wood or charcoal is burned to heat the kiln.

3

Kylix

Drinking cups have big handles to make them easy to hold by people lying on couches. These three shapes are the most popular.

Skyphos

Kantharos

From a *krater*, diluted wine is transferred into a jug called an *oinochoe*, above, ready to be poured into wine cups.

Black-figured decoration

The same image as red-figured decoration

Making black and red figure ware

The Athenians use two types of pottery decoration. The first, black-figure ware, fashionable from about 550–480 BCE, and then red-figure ware, developed after 530 BCE. The red-figure technique is more sophisticated but harder to paint. In both techniques the artist paints what will be black in the finished pot, so on a red-figured pot the details are created by not painting them, that is painting around them making a drawing in reverse.

The areas that will be black are painted with a mixture of clay, water and wood ash. Small details can be scratched in this "slip" to let the red show through. At a certain point in the firing process, the kiln's vents are shut. This cuts off the oxygen supply and causes a chemical reaction that turns the whole pot black. When the temperature drops and the vents are reopened, the areas painted black stay black, but the rest of the pot turns a clear red color.

A *krater* is a large vase for mixing wine with water before serving. The one above is a volute krater.

Crafts and Trades—Sculpture

The visitor to ancient Greece cannot help but notice how many statues greet the eye at every turn. These sculptures depict many different subjects, but most importantly the human form.

Statues are used to decorate temples and people's homes, to commemorate famous men legendary and real, and to mark graves. Five materials are used for sculpting—clay, terracotta (which means "baked earth"), wood, bronze, and stone (usually limestone or marble).

The mountainous nature of Greece means that there is plenty of stone available, but it is difficult to transport from the quarries to the sculptors' workshops in the cities. Large blocks are usually cut in the quarry to the rough shape of the statue, to reduce its size and weight. The detailed carving is then done in a workshop.

A finished statue is painted in lifelike colors, and sometimes colored glass, stone, or ivory is inlaid for the eyes. Details such as garlands, crowns, weapons, or horse tackle are made of hammered or cast bronze and fitted onto the stone.

Below: In a busy studio, ready sculptures are painted. The finished work of the sculptor in the foreground may be seen on page 74.

Reconstruction of the giant statue of Athena in the Parthenon, created by Phidias. Given the scale, it is amazing to think it was made from ivory and gold.

Small versions of Athena made in clay are popular souvenirs with visitors to Athens.

Wood, bronze, and terracotta

Wooden statues and carvings are suitable for decorating a home, but because the wood soon decays, it is not a popular material for exterior use. Bronze statues are made in three different ways (*see page 60*).

Terracotta is not suitable for large pieces, and is mostly used for small figurines and plaques for temples and homes. Perhaps because of the material's humble nature, the most popular figurines depict scenes of everyday life—barbers at work, a butcher cutting meat, scenes in the home, and so on.

A superbly realistic racing horse of bronze.

Early Greek sculptors copied Egyptian poses for statues of young men, called *kouroi*. As they became more lifelike, there was an interest in the nude female form as well.

Clay toys

Although making figurines from clay is a part of the potters' art, there are potters who specialise in this craft and rarely make pots. Clay statuettes are both handmade and turned out in quantity from baked clay molds. The variety is astonishing. Figures of horses—with and without riders—and dogs are popular. Dolls, models of boats and articles of food, miniature pots, household furniture, even tiny roof tiles and mirrors may be found on the modeler's well-stacked shelves, ready for sale to a doting parent to delight his children.

Plaques in relief portraying deities, priestesses, and warriors are mass-produced for votive offerings at temples, especially those of Asclepius, the god of healing (*see page 86*).

The picture below, based on a Corinthian factory, shows the model-maker pressing clay into a mold. A mold for a doll's torso and finished examples can be seen beside his hands. An arrangement of painted figurines stands on the table to the left. A boy carries a tray of finished figurines to the storage shelves under their protective roof.

Crafts and Trades—Metalworkers

The craftsmen who work in metals have their quarter near the temple of their patron god, Hephaestus. Here, the air rings with the clamor of hammering and smelting from the numerous small and large workshops.

Bronze

Copper arrives from Cyprus and the eastern Mediterranean, and tin from the mines of Spain, Brittany, and even far away Cornwall in England. When the two are smelted together, the bronze alloy is the result.

Bronze is used for many everyday items such as kitchen utensils and ladies' mirrors. It is also a popular medium for statues. Early statues were made from sheets of bronze hammered over a wooden frame; later, small statues were made from solid metal cast in molds.

The "lost-wax" casting method is used for small statues and especially for large ones where the final weight of the finished product is greatly reduced by being hollow, such as the 4th-century bronze horse seen on the previous page.

In this, a rough shape is made in clay. Bronze pins are inserted and a detailed wax model is built around the clay core. The wax model is then covered by an outer clay mold. Next, the clay molds are fired in a kiln and the heat melts away the wax model, leaving a perfect impression of its shape on the inside of the outer mold (the inserted bronze pins keep the central core in place as the wax melts).

Next, molten bronze is poured in between the outer mold and the inner core, and when it has cooled, the outer clay mold is cracked away to reveal the finished bronze figure. The inner clay core is broken and removed through a small hole in the statue's base. Bronze is also used to make military armor (*see pages 78–79*), but for weapons such as swords and spearheads, iron is a much tougher metal.

Iron

Iron is more useful than bronze when it comes to edged tools and weapons, as it can be made harder and sharper. It was first used in Greece in about 1050 BCE, but since then manufacturing techniques have improved. In iron-making, the furnace needs to be a much higher temperature than for bronze.

Making statues by hammering bronze over wood.

The bronze "Vix *krater*" (named after the French town where it was discovered) is huge. At 5.4 feet high, it weighs 458 pounds, and holds an amazing 317 gallons of wine—enough for more than 20 symposiums!

Above: Smelting iron.

Left: A gold thumb ring with scenes of a fertility rite.

Right: A gold chest made to hold the funerary ashes of King Philip II of Macedon, father of Alexander the Great.

Gold and silver

Precious metals are used to make jewelry, luxury goods, and coins. Some statues are made of ivory and gold, such as the statue of Athena in the Parthenon illustrated on page 58. The most widespread use of silver is in minting coins (*see page 66*).

Silver is mined at Laurion, near Athens, and the city owns the workings, which are leased out to private contractors. The conditions are dreadful, with miners working shifts of up to ten hours. The philosopher Aristotle defines slaves as "possessions that breathe, tools that happen to be alive," and the unluckiest slaves in Greece are those forced to mine for silver at Laurion (*below*).

Down the mine

1. Ventilation shaft

2. Vertical access shafts less than 6ft wide lead down into the mine. The miners use wooden ladders.

3. Ore is hauled up to the surface in a basket suspended from a roller.

4. Rock pillars are left to support the roof.

5. Oil lamps provide illumination.

6. Miners use chisels and hammers.

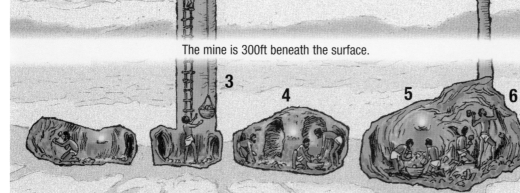

The mine is 300ft beneath the surface.

Crafts and Trades—Carpentry and Architecture

Carpenters are divided into two trades—domestic and structural, the first making furniture, the second a vital part of the architect's craft.

Most furniture in a Greek home is made from wood, and its style varies little between the poor and the wealthy—rich people just have more ornate and highly decorated furniture. The finest pieces are intricately carved, and probably have inlays of ivory, gold, and silver. Items such as lampstands are made of bronze, with pottery lamps on top.

Seating
The commonest seat is a stool, with either fixed or folding legs and a leather or woven cloth seat.

The *klismos* is a chair with a back, popular with ladies.

Tables
Tables come in several shapes and sizes, but they are usually low so that they can be pushed under couches when not in use. Most tables have three legs or a central pedestal support.

The head of the family sits on a *thronos*, a large chair with a back and arms. The back is padded, as is the comfortable seat.

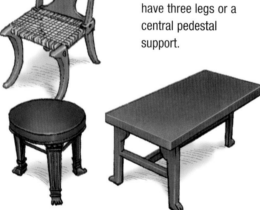

Couches and beds
Beds and the dining couches called *anaklintra* are similar in design. Leather strips or woven cords are strung across the wooden bed frame. A mattress and cushions are placed on top, and beds have a cover.

Storage
Wood is used for a variety of chests and smaller boxes to hold personal items ranging from jewelry to clothes and bed linen.

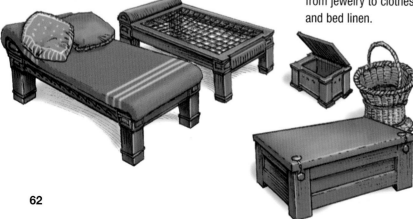

The architect's skill

Domestic architecture is of little interest to the Greeks and private houses are relatively simple affairs of mud brick. Instead, the Greeks devote themselves to public buildings. These provide a focus for both civic pride and religious feelings—and the more there are, the greater the city's status. A description of architectural styles and the separate elements of a Greek temple may be found on pages 24–25.

However, the construction of these public monuments owes a great deal to the engineering skills of carpenters, who must build the scaffolding and erect the lifting engines. And when the building is almost complete, they are called on to provide the roof frame and ceilings, which are usually made of wood.

A public building essentially consists of stone blocks and stone columns. Limestone and marble are the normal materials, but softer sandstone is also used in the western colonies. The roughly hewn blocks arrive from the quarry, and are shaped on the ground by masons using hammers and chisels.

Columns are made of cylindrical pieces of stone, called drums. The fluting grooves are started while each drum is still on the ground and only finished when an entire column (of normally 11 drums) is in place.

Ropes and pulleys are used to haul the heavy stone blocks to the building height. They are then maneuvered into place with levers. Each block has a pre-made groove cut into its ends so it can be joined to the next block by means of a piece of metal called a cramp. It is joined to the cramps above and below it with metal rods called dowels.

Column drums are also lifted by a block-and-tackle pulley system. When the drum is being prepared on the ground, the mason leaves four spurs sticking out, and ropes are passed around these for lifting. Once in place, the stone spurs are knocked off.

When the blocks and drums are in place, apprentice masons go around and polish their surfaces with a hard stone and a lubricant.

Common types of public building

A *stoa*, or porch, is a building forming a walkway on one or two floors, with open colonnades at the front, often used for shops or offices.

Altars stood in the open air, usually in front of a temple, for purposes of public worship and sacrifice. Most were simple stone slabs, but could be as ornate as the one **above**.

A *tholos* is a round building or temple with a conical roof. In Athens the *prytani* meet in the Tholos (*see page 71*).

Right: Votive statues are erected to honor famous events or heroes.

Above: Treasuries are small temple-like buildings at sanctuaries used for storing valuable offerings, such as war booty in honor of a god.

A *propylaea*, or propylon, is an elaborate gateway to a religious sanctuary, such as the one on the Acropolis of Athens.

Building a temple

Two workmen at the right lower the final drum of a column into position. The lower drum has a block of wood set in its center to aid in alignment. The columns are set up with only rough fluting, which is finished afterward to ensure precision jointing. The lifting spurs will be knocked off once the drum is firmly in place. In the foreground, other workers maneuver a block into position, while a third gives the blocks a fine finish. The metal I-shaped cramps securing the unmortared blocks are clearly visible.

CHAPTER 4

Peace and War

Heart of the Polis—the Agora

The Greek *agora*, or marketplace, is a natural place for exchanging gossip, debating matters of state, and for public discussion. It is the center of trade and of politics, where the government meets and from where wars are conducted.

At the heart of every Greek city is the *agora*. It is the center of a city's commercial life, and a social focus where people gather to meet friends. The finest *agora* in all Greece is found in Athens, which was once the place where an ancient race track existed for the annual religious games. Gradually, it developed into a market, and

from there to the political hub of the city.

Farmers from the surrounding region still come to the central open space, erect their stalls, and sell meat, poultry, fish, vegetables, cheese, fruit, and eggs. Around the edges craftsmen have their numerous workshops, while here and there knots of men looking for work gather in spots where employers are known to hire for particular trades.

The political hub

To the east and south are the great *stoas*, or porches, colonnaded arcades that offer welcome shade and also provide space for small shops and business offices. The shops are open rooms with a counter across the front, and since they cost more to rent than a market stall, they tend to sell luxury goods.

On the western side of the *agora* sit the various government buildings that house the *Boule* (see below and page 71) and the *Strategion*. This is the center of the Athenian military command. In times of war, the *Boule* appoints a supreme commander—the *strategos*—who is responsible for the navy and the army. In other times, there were a number of *strategoi*, who acted as generals.

Together with altars and temples, you have in one place the essence of a Greek city.

The Agora of Athens

buildings c.500 BCE
buildings c.380 BCE
buildings c.200 BCE

painted stoa
to Dipylon Gate
Panathenaic Way
N
royal stoa
Archaic Period building
altar of the Olympian gods
stoa of Zeus
shops
shops
Eschara
old law court
B
temple of Hephaestus
seats
temple of Apollo
Archaic Period racetrack
square peristyle
Colonos Agoraeos (Agora Hill)
Old Bouleuterion
stoa of Attalus (built over earlier houses and shops)
metalworkers quarter
A
New Bouleuterion
C
Panathenaic Way
Tholos
Archaic Period building
east building
to Acropolis
Strategion (army HQ)
middle stoa
B
southwest fountain house
Hellaea
south square
new south stoa
shoemaker's shop
triangular shrine
mint
old south stoa
SE fountain house
prison
Areopagus
six houses of the Classic Period

0   100   200 ft
0   50   100 m

Key to a city's commercial heart

A Athens is governed by an assembly of 500 elected members—called the *Boule*—who meet in the New and Old *Bouleuterion*. A "steering committee" of 50 selected *Boule* members, called the *prytani*, meets in the circular Tholos, which also houses the official weights and standard measures.

B The old law court (top right) fell into disuse early on and cases are heard in the Hellaea, which is incorporated in the new south stoa.

C The ancient race track has disappeared under the *agora*'s center, which is filled with market stalls and small stores.

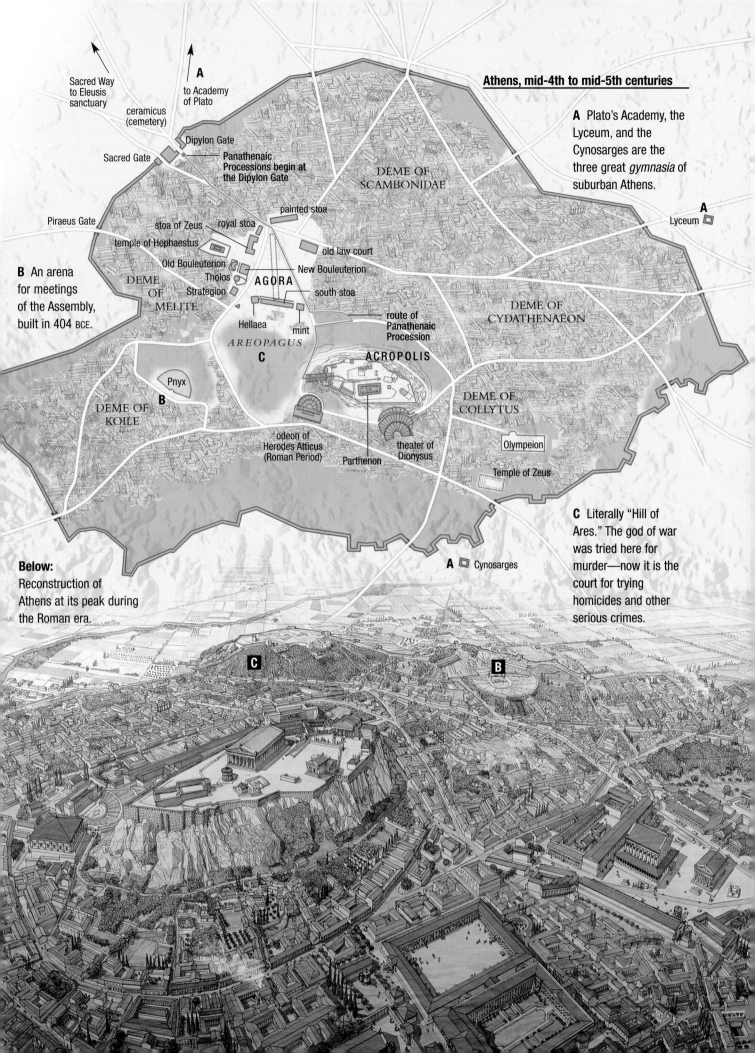

Sacred Way
to Eleusis
sanctuary

ceramicus
(cemetery)

to Academy
of Plato

Dipylon Gate

Sacred Gate

**Panathenaic
Processions begin at
the Dipylon Gate**

Piraeus Gate

painted stoa

stoa of Zeus   royal stoa

temple of Hephaestus

old law court

Old Bouleuterion   New Bouleuterion

Tholos

B An arena
for meetings
of the Assembly,
built in 404 BCE.

DEME
OF
MELITE

Strategion

AGORA

south stoa

Hellaea   mint

AREOPAGUS

C

route of
Panathenaic
Procession

DEME OF
SCAMBONIDAE

Athens, mid-4th to mid-5th centuries

A Plato's Academy, the
Lyceum, and the
Cynosarges are the
three great *gymnasia* of
suburban Athens.

A

Lyceum

DEME OF
CYDATHENAEON

ACROPOLIS

Pnyx

B

DEME OF
KOILE

odeon of
Herodes Atticus
(Roman Period)

Parthenon

theater of
Dionysus

DEME OF
COLLYTUS

Olympeion

Temple of Zeus

A Cynosarges

C Literally "Hill of
Ares." The god of war
was tried here for
murder—now it is the
court for trying
homicides and other
serious crimes.

Below:
Reconstruction of
Athens at its peak during
the Roman era.

C

B

Money Makes Trade Easier

Neither Mesopotamians nor Egyptians used coins for trade, but the Greeks do. While a barter system still operates in poorer rural regions, coinage is the currency of the *agora*.

The first coins arrived a long time ago at the end of the 7th century BCE from a small state called Lydia, in Asia Minor. With their capital at Sardis, the Lydians traded with the Greeks of the Ionian coast, and from there the use of coins spread to all of Greece and its colonies.

Early coins made of electrum—a naturally occurring alloy of gold and silver—may still be found in circulation in backward places, but most coins are made of gold or silver, which guarantees the purity of each coin.

It is a matter of pride for a Greek city-state to mint its own coins, which is a sign of its independence. The only exception to this used to be Sparta, which continued to use iron rods instead of coins until the 4th century BCE.

Greek coins

Coin from Aegina, c.560 BCE. The sea turtle is associated with the cult of Hera. It has a simple stamp on the back.

Obverse (front)

Reverse (back)

The first Greek coins were stamped from lumps of electrum with the symbol of the issuing polis to show that their weight and purity were guaranteed by the state.

A silver *tetradrachm* from Eretria, c.525 BCE. Eretria was one of the first Greek mints to strike coins in silver rather than electrum. This face is the reverse, which depicts a squid.

In 600–480 BCE animals most commonly appeared on coins, usually the symbol of the issuing *polis* or associated with the city's main religious cult.

Obverse (front)

Silver coin from Syracuse, 413 BCE, showing a chariot on the front and the head of the nymph Arethusa and dolphins, the city's symbols.

Reverse (back)

Left: Gold *stater* of Philip II of Macedon, 359–36 BCE. **Right:** silver coin showing Alexander the Great, 334 BCE.

After 480 BCE, the human face and intricate scenes began to appear, due to better minting techniques.

In the Hellenistic Period, coin quality improved and heads of rulers began to appear.

Standardizing weights and measures

The city-state ensures people shopping in the *agora* are not cheated by its traders. At Athens, the official standard weights and measures are kept in the Tholos, the circular building next to the Bouleuterion. From here, the various officials take their weights and measuring jars into the *agora* to check against those being used by traders.

Ten *metronomoi* are chosen annually to check the weights and measures. Their

Above: A standard measure jar and, **right**, a typical trader's stone weight.

colleagues, the *agoranomoi*, check the quality of goods on sale, and the *sitophylakes* look after the grain trade. The grain trade is so vital to the economy—since Athens has to import two-thirds of what it needs from the Greek colonies—that it is a capital offense to be caught exporting any grain.

The business of
changing money is
usually done by *Metics*,
or foreign residents.
They are happy that the
fiercely independent
Greek city-states all
issue their own coinage
because the money-
changers make a profit
on every transaction.

Money exchange and banking

The insistence of cities to issue their own
coinage means that merchants who want to
trade with another city have to go to a
money changer before any business can be
done. They earn their keep by charging a fee
for exchanging one currency for another.

In the *agora* of every city, money-
changers—called *trapezitae*, or "table men"—
can be found at their distinctive tables
touting for business. Competition is steep,
with each attempting to offer better rates of
exchange than their neighbors. Despite this,
trapezitae do very well, and some have
become so rich that they can afford to lend
money to merchants and citizens.

In Athens, privately owned *trapezae*, or

banks, have become an essential part of long-
distance trade. To feed its citizens the city
requires hundreds of ship cargoes. Almost all
of these cargoes are dependent on loans.

Because the *trapezae* have arrangements
with fellow bankers in distant ports, a
merchant can travel with a trusted guarantee
from his own bank to pay the seller's bank at
the other end, in return for paying interest
on his loan. In this way he avoids the
dangers and inconvenience of transporting
large and heavy amounts of cash with him.

The innovation of banking has
revolutionized trade, and made Athens and
its port of Piraeus the most important
mercantile centers in the Mediterranean.

Merchant Shipping and Travel

The mountainous nature of mainland Greece, its far-flung colonies and island territories, and the almost perpetual war between the Greek states, makes sea travel the most practical way of getting about.

There are many safe harbors along the Greek coasts, and most merchant-captains are happy to take fees for carrying passengers. Sea travel has its risks, however. Storms are common—and so are shipwrecks. Ships can be stranded from lack of wind or driven off course. Pirates are a plague; and unscrupulous captains have been known to rob their passengers once they have put out to sea.

The sensible sea-voyager lines up at the altar near the harbor to make a sacrifice to Poseidon to ensure a successful trip.

The merchant ship

Few merchant ships have much of a superstructure, so there is no accommodation, although the captain might fit out a small cabin for himself on a larger vessel. Merchant ships are not large, so they rarely sail during bad weather. Shipping hugs the shores to be close to land should a storm arise, and to put in at night, with the crew and any passengers sleeping on the beach.

Metics and slaves

Foreigners living and working in Greek cities (which includes Greeks from other city-states) are called *Metics*. They form an essential part of the state—Athens alone has 25,000 *Metics*. The majority are merchants—few Athenians enter into mercantile trade themselves—who manage the shipping and import businesses that make Athens rich. *Metics* also include artisans, physicians, philosophers, teachers, and leading artists.

However, although *Metics* as non-citizens are not allowed to own property or land, and may not vote, they pay taxes and can be called up for military service in times of need.

Slaves come below *Metics*, but they also form a vital part of the economic and social structure. There may be as many as 100,000 slaves in Athens and Attica—roughly half of the entire population. Elsewhere, slaves are not so numerous.

A merchant ship equipped with oars as well as a sail is called a *kerkouros*. It usually has a ram at the prow (front) to fight pirate ships.

Timber for ship-building is scarce in most of Greece, so the pine for the hull structure and the flexible spruce for the mast comes from Thrace, Macedonia, or Phoenicia (Lebanon).

The trade in slaves is a busy one. Slaves come from all over the known world, but particularly from around the shores of the Black Sea, Thrace, the Middle East, and along the coast of Asia Minor.

Most slaves are well treated and have some rights under Athenian law. They may even have an income, and their ranks include highly skilled craftsmen. However, slaves employed in the silver mines of Laurion work in terrible conditions where their life expectancy is very short.

Large *amphorae* are carefully designed to allow for tight stacking in multiple layers. At its destination, the amphora can be stood upright in loose sand.

Flax or hemp ropes are tied to the square sail's cleats (deck fittings).

Ships are steered by two rudders at the stern (back).

Cargo is stored below the covered deck.

Land travel

The good roads in Greece usually only connect a city with the neighboring religious centers, such as Athens and Eleusis. The rest are in poor condition, most barely more than tracks, and there are hardly any bridges spanning rivers, which means land travel is hard. Taking into account the continual wars between states and the brigands who control the lonelier areas, and overland journeys are also dangerous.

Oxen-drawn carts are used over short distances, and usually near a major town where the road surface might be reasonable. Longer distances require donkeys or mules, accustomed to carrying heavy weights over poor and hilly terrain.

For most travelers a journey means going on foot, in groups to deter bandit attacks, or well armed if alone. Major routes offer some inns for overnight accommodation, but they provide only a bed, not meals, which means travelers must carry food supplies in addition to any other baggage. Travelers may arrange to stay with relatives along their route, and in towns they can sleep under the colonnades of public buildings.

The *diolkos* of Corinth

Although the isthmus of Corinth is narrow, the height of the rocky land makes it impossible to dig a canal. Instead, the clever Corinthians have constructed a *diolkos*—a paved slipway—connecting the Saronic Gulf to the Gulf of Corinth. This cuts over 185 nautical miles off a ship's journey between the Aegean and Adriatic Seas.

Ships are borne by slaves across the isthmus on a wheeled vehicle called an *olkos*. The *diolkos* itself is a 10-foot wide pavement of limestone blocks.

A section of the *diolkos*, showing the pavement heavily grooved by the wheels of the ship-bearing *olkos*.

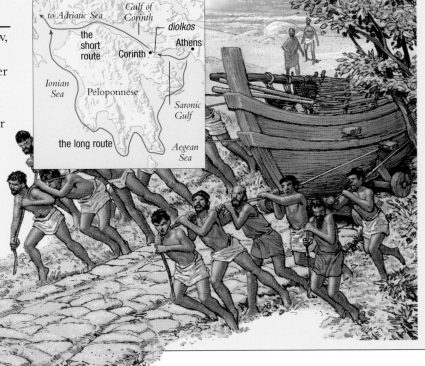

to Adriatic Sea

Gulf of Corinth

diolkos

the short route

Corinth

Athens

Ionian Sea

Peloponnese

Saronic Gulf

the long route

Aegean Sea

Democracy, Greek Style

The city-state, or *polis* of Athens has evolved the most sophisticated form of government anywhere in the known world—*demos-kratos*, or people-power—and all other Greek states except Sparta would like to imitate it.

Thanks to the political reforms of the statesman Cleisthenes (c.570–c.508 BCE), Athenians enjoy democracy and have the right to vote on administrative matters and to run for election to public office. However, only registered citizens of the *polis* enjoy this right—all other social groups, such as women, *Metics*, and slaves, are excluded. A citizen must belong to a local community of Attica and be registered with his tribe.

The local organization of Attica

Based on the reorganization of Cleisthenes, Attica (Athens and the surrounding area), is divided into 170 *demes* (local communities), each with its own *demarchos* (mayor) and local government. All eligible voters are listed according to their *deme*, even if they move to another part of the state.

According to ancient custom, each man also belongs to a *phyle*, or tribe. In Attica there are ten *phylae*, each named for a legendary hero of Attica's history. The *phylae* are political

A member of the *Boule* has a hard time persuading the *ekklesia* of a new law's benefits. In the foreground, latecomers' tunics are marked by red dye from the ropes that slaves use to round them up— absence is not tolerated.

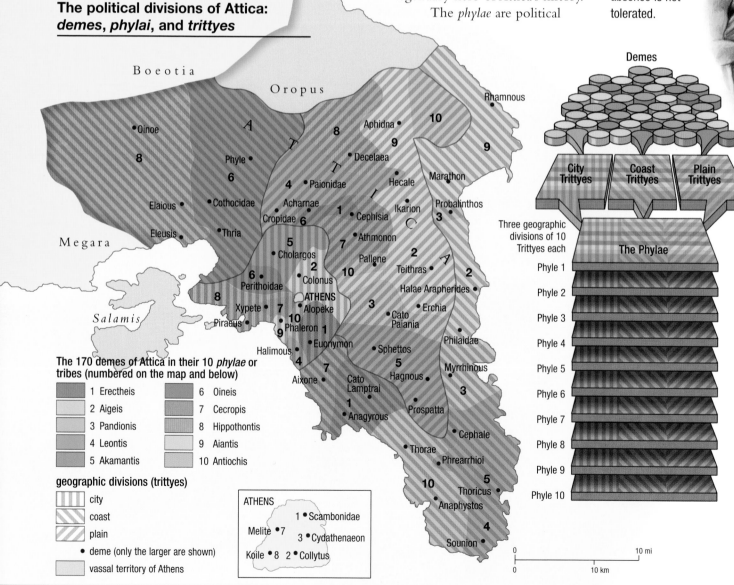

The political divisions of Attica: demes, phylai, and trittyes

The 170 demes of Attica in their 10 *phylae* or tribes (numbered on the map and below)

1 Erectheis
2 Aigeis
3 Pandionis
4 Leontis
5 Akamantis
6 Oineis
7 Cecropis
8 Hippothontis
9 Aiantis
10 Antiochis

geographic divisions (trittyes)

city
coast
plain
deme (only the larger are shown)
vassal territory of Athens

Demes

City Trittyes | Coast Trittyes | Plain Trittyes

Three geographic divisions of 10 Trittyes each

The Phylae

Phyle 1
Phyle 2
Phyle 3
Phyle 4
Phyle 5
Phyle 6
Phyle 7
Phyle 8
Phyle 9
Phyle 10

ATHENS
1 Scambonidae
Melite 7
3 Cydathenaeon
Koile 8 2 Collytus

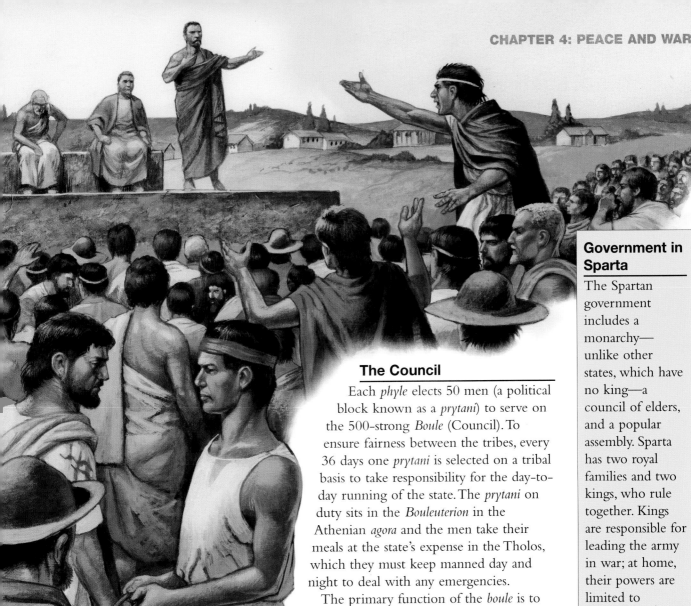

Government in Sparta

The Spartan government includes a monarchy—unlike other states, which have no king—a council of elders, and a popular assembly. Sparta has two royal families and two kings, who rule together. Kings are responsible for leading the army in war; at home, their powers are limited to religious duties.

The *gerousia* (council) is made up of the two kings and 20 councillors, men over the age of 60 who are elected for life by the *apella*, or Assembly. The *apella* consists of all citizens over the age of 30. Unlike the Athenian *Ekklesia*, the *Apella* cannot debate or amend a measure submitted by the *gerousia*, only vote "yes" or "no."

The Council

Each *phyle* elects 50 men (a political block known as a *prytani*) to serve on the 500-strong *Boule* (Council). To ensure fairness between the tribes, every 36 days one *prytani* is selected on a tribal basis to take responsibility for the day-to-day running of the state. The *prytani* on duty sits in the *Bouleuterion* in the Athenian *agora* and the men take their meals at the state's expense in the Tholos, which they must keep manned day and night to deal with any emergencies.

The primary function of the *boule* is to draw up new laws and policies to put to the Assembly of the people.

The Assembly

Every citizen has the right to speak and to vote at the *ekklesia*, or Assembly, which meets about once every ten days on a hill called the Pnyx (*see also the map on page 65*). The *ekklesia* debates proposals put forward by the council, and decisions such as the allocation of public money, declaration of war, or the forming of an alliance are decided by the vote.

Of course, not every one of the 40,000 citizens in Attica can get to the Pnyx every time there is a vote, and the usual number present is more like the minimum 6000 necessary for a vote to take place. If too few people attend, slaves in the state's pay are sent out in groups holding ropes dipped in red paint to round up latecomers and shirkers. Anyone found with red paint on his clothes is shamed and fined.

units, since each *phyle* is given *demes* in approximately equal proportion. This creates ten political blocks, each containing approximately 17 local *demes*.

The *demes* within each tribe are further divided into *trittyes* (thirds), based on three geographical groupings: City, Coast, or Plain (inland Attica). The result of this elegant division is that each *deme* contains a cross-section of the people, both urban and rural.

Because the *phylae* are scattered across Attica, they have to cooperate with their fellow *phylae* in different locations to safeguard their collective tribal interests. The system is complicated, but the map on the left helps to explain how it works.

A Democrat's Duties

The freedom to vote on the state's direction and policies brings additional responsibilities. It is every citizen's duty to take an active part in how the government and legal system operates.

The three most important of the nine *archons* of Athens, clockwise from the top left: *Basileus, Eponymous*, and *Polemarch*.

The great *strategos* and gifted politician Pericles, who used the Delian League's fighting funds to beautify Athens.

Below: The *strategos* Themistocles leads the Athenian army against the Persian invaders.

The *archons*

Nine officials or ministers called *archons* are selected annually by lot from among the citizens to prepare legal cases for trial in the *ekklesia* and organize religious ceremonies. Three *archons* are more important than the others and have special duties.

The *Polemarch Archon* is charged to deal with the legal affairs of Metics. He is also in charge of games and offerings in honor of men killed in battle.

The *Eponymous Archon* chooses the men who are to finance the choral and drama contests of the Dionysian festival (*see pages 90–91*). He also handles lawsuits involving inheritance.

The most senior, the *Basileus Archon*, presides over the court specially set up to try murder cases, which hears cases on the Areopagus hill. He also arranges religious sacrifices, rents out temple lands, and supervises the Dionysia.

The *strategoi*

The highest-ranking state officials are the ten *strategoi*, or generals, one representing each *phyle*, elected by the citizens. Holding office for a year—though he can be re-elected many times—a *strategos* wields immense power over both the army and the economy, implements decisions voted on by the *Boule* abroad and at home, and acts as an ambassador to other Greek states and foreign countries. A *strategos* answers to the Assembly for his actions and for the money he spends.

The power of Pericles

The most famous *strategos* is Pericles, leader of Athens in the mid-5th century. He took power after the Persian Wars and forged an alliance of friendly cities into an Athenian empire. This was known as the Delian League because its treasury was initially kept on the island of Delos. But Pericles contrived to have it moved to Athens, where it is kept in the Parthenon—one of the many fine buildings Pericles had built with the league's money.

The law

It is every citizen's duty to participate in the running of the legal system, and they exercise great power through the law courts. *Strategoi* who lose battles can be brought to trial to account for their failures. Petty litigation is widespread, especially over property and inheritances.

All citizens over the age of 30 are expected to volunteer for jury service. A small payment is made by the state to make up for lost earnings and to ensure that even poorer citizens may take part. There are no attorneys or judges, but a presiding *archon* sees that a case is properly tried, while offering no opinion on the matter.

A minimum of 201 jurors is required at a trial, selected from the volunteers using a *kleroteria* machine. Each side is then allowed equal time to present its case. This is measured against a water clock, and when a speaker's time has run out, he has to stop immediately.

Each juror is given two bronze disks, one with a solid center (innocent), the other hollow in the middle (guilty). At the trial's end, the jurors hand the appropriate disk to an official and a simple majority decides the accused's fate.

Justice is administered by the city officials, and punishments include death, mutilation, imprisonment, house arrest, fining, and exile.

Pot punishment—ostracism

Exile is a common means of punishing criminals and getting rid of unpopular figures—usually politicians. A vote of ostracism is held once every year in the Assembly. Each citizen who attends scratches the name of the person he wants to see exiled on a piece of broken pottery, called an *ostrakon*.

A minimum of 6000 votes is required for a man to be banished, or "ostracized," and the unlucky citizen has to leave Athens within ten days and remain in exile for ten years.

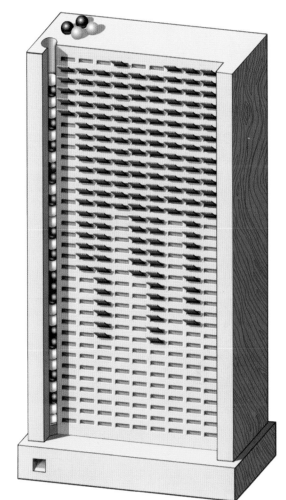

A *kleroteria* machine stands outside every court, which is used to select jurors. Athenian citizens place bronze identification tickets called *pinakia* in the slots. Black and white balls dropped randomly into a tube at the side determine which row of citizens will serve on a jury for the day.

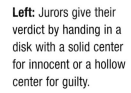

Left: Jurors give their verdict by handing in a disk with a solid center for innocent or a hollow center for guilty.

Themistocles was ostracized when he fell out of favor with powerful politicians. The *ostrakon* pictured here is one that a citizen handed in as his vote to exile the *strategos*.

Athletics—Training for War

Athletics have a religious significance to the Greeks, but since every citizen must be ready to take up arms for his city when called, maintaining a regime of physical exercise is a duty as well as a pleasure.

The Greek passion for athleticism is rooted in civic pride and the idea that fitness is a civic responsibility. From the age of 12, every son of a citizen is expected to become proficient in all manner of athletic sports, training with his *gymnasium* (*see pages 49–51*). Soldiers (or future soldiers) need to be in prime physical condition to fight for their *polis*. The sporting arenas and *gymnasia* are an alternative to the barracks square, and the emphasis on physical training ensures that the majority of young males will be fit enough to fight.

The sculptor Myron's *Discobolus* is a superb image of the Greek pentathlete.

Foot races

Being swift of foot is essential for any soldier, whether in charging an enemy or fleeing to fight another day. For this reason, running is the oldest sporting event. Youths train for three main races based on the length of the standard Greek *stadion* (stadium), which is about 600 feet long. The *stade* is one length, the *diaulos* two lengths, and the mammoth *dolichos* 20–24 lengths.

Skill contests

Throwing the discus and javelin form part of the standard pentathlon competition and rarely feature as standalone events. Javelins are equipped with a thong wound around the shaft. This gives the missile a rotary motion that makes it fly a greater distance. There are two kinds of javelin event: throwing for distance and throwing at a target from horseback. The long jump is another part of the *pentathlon*. To extend the length of the jump the competitor carries a weight in each hand which he swings while running along the ramp. The weights are released just before landing.

Pentathlon

This contest consists of five events: running, wrestling, the long jump, and discus- and javelin-throwing. It is designed to find the best all-around athlete, and requires great stamina. One of Greece's most famous sculptures is of a pentathlete throwing the discus.

Pankration

This combination of boxing and wrestling is very rough. It is not unusual for *pankration* athletes to be seriously injured or even killed. The event involves a series of paired fights that continue until one of the athletes concedes. Almost anything is allowed except gouging the eyes and biting. Soldiers are usually the best at this sport.

Equestrian events

The basic horse race is run over a distance of about three-quarters of a mile. Jockeys ride bareback and accidents are common.

Chariot races for teams of two or four horses with one rider consist of 12 laps. As many as 40 chariots take part, so exciting collisions are frequent. Equestrian events are exclusive to the aristocratic and wealthy because entrants must own their horses.

Wrestling and boxing

The object in wrestling is to throw the opponent so that his shoulder touches the ground, while the adversary remains on his feet. The first man to fall three times loses. Tripping is allowed, but no punching. Boxers bind their hands with soft ox-hide thongs for protection. A contest can go on for several hours and ends when one boxer concedes defeat or loses consciousness. In both events opponents are chosen at random, so athletes of different weights and sizes may find themselves matched.

Fact box

The marathon is a modern race. It was conceived for the 1896 Olympics in Athens, first Olympics of the modern era. The race is said to commemorate the 26-mile run from Marathon to Athens made by a messenger in 490 BCE to inform the Boule that the Athenian army had defeated the Persians at the battle of Marathon.

The winners

Prizes given in many festival games such as the Panathenaic are financially rewarding. But in panhellenic events such as the Olympics athletes seek only the honor of taking part and the glory of winning. Winners are presented with an olive wreath, palm branches, and woolen ribbons.

To add to their prestige in the games, some cities are happy to sponsor successful sportsmen, and some athletes make a decent living in this way.

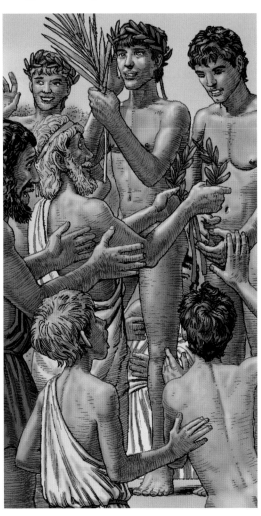

Cheats never prosper

Cheating does sometimes occur. The first recorded Olympic cheat was Eupolus of Thessaly who, in 384 BC, tried to fix his boxing bout by bribing the judges. Some cities bribe others' athletes to throw a race or discus shot. If a city is caught the heavy fine is used to erect statues of Zeus along the road leading to Olympia. Individual cheats have their names inscribed on plaques at the athletes' entrance to the stadium.

International Peace—the Olympic Games

The Greeks celebrate several panhellenic games, involving competitors from across the country and its colonies, but the most prestigious are those held in honor of Zeus every four years at Olympia.

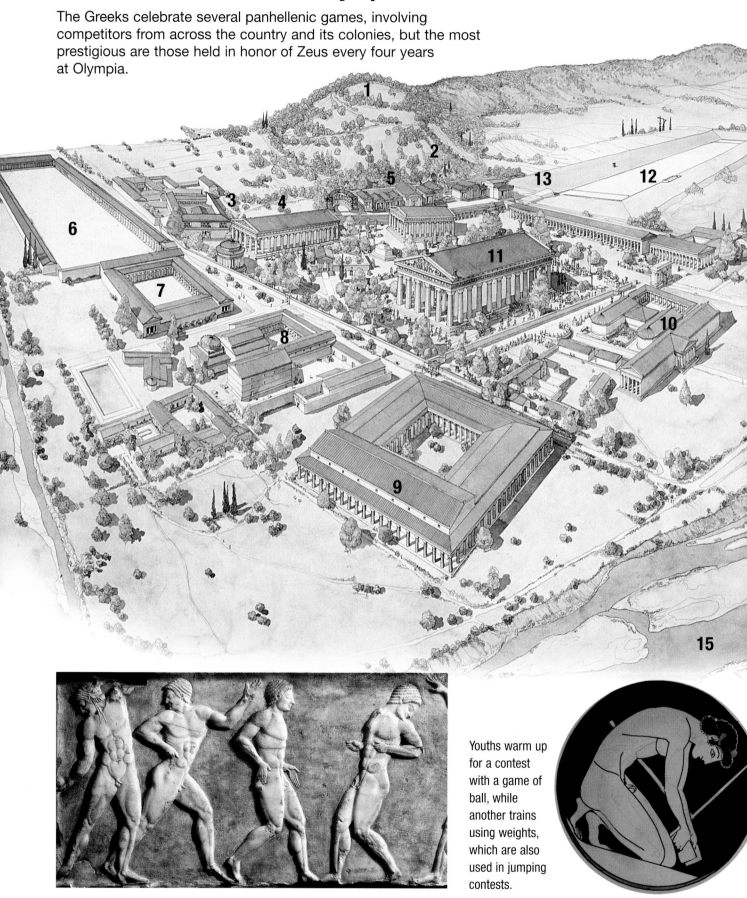

Youths warm up for a contest with a game of ball, while another trains using weights, which are also used in jumping contests.

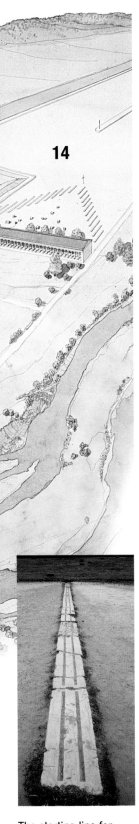

14

The starting line for foot-races in the *stadion*.

In the year of the Olympic Games, messengers travel all over Greece and the colonies, announcing the date of the games and inviting people to attend. In this sacred festival, athletes perform for the gods as much as for their city-state or themselves. Athletic prowess is venerated, and Olympian heroes are honored throughout the Greek world.

At the announcement all wars must stop to allow competitors and spectators to travel to Olympia and return home in safety. And so for a few short weeks, the quarrelsome Greek city-states bond into a united whole.

A mystical place of peace

Olympia, situated in the northwestern Peloponnese, is recognized as a non-political sanctuary. It sits in the sacred wood of Altis, beneath the Hill of Cronus, named after the father of Zeus. It is a place of mystery, myth, religion, and legend—a fitting venue for sporting heroes.

Olympia is an impressive complex specially built for the games, at the heart of which stands the great Temple of Zeus.

No women allowed

The athletes compete in the nude, as they do at the *gymnasium*, and for this reason no women may compete or even attend the games. In fact, no woman may approach Olympia during the games (*see "Other panhellenic games"*).

Chariot racing is the only event a woman may win if she owns a horse. She may not actually race or be present to watch her jockey take part. However, if her horse wins, she will eventually receive the prize.

The order of events

Religious festivals and diplomatic gatherings flank the central sporting events, so the celebrations last for almost two weeks.

On the first day the opening ceremony involves religious celebrations and sacrifices to the gods. On the second day the *stadion* race is held, the most prestigious contest of the games. The *stadion*, surrounded by banks capable of seating about 40,000 spectators, serves as the focal point for most of the Olympic events.

Over the next three days the *pentathlon*, wrestling, boxing, *pankration*, and equestrian events are held, finishing with the *dolichos* running race. When the last event has been held, the prizes all awarded, the religious celebrations concluded, the brief moment of bonding and unity is over, and it is time to pick up the many wars where they left off.

Other panhellenic games

The Isthmian Games are held every two years in the isthmus of Corinth. The location is symbolically important, representing the unity of the Peloponnesian Greeks with fellow Greeks to the north. The Pythian Games are held in Delphi every four years and are the second-largest sporting event after the Olympics.

A separate festival for women, the Heraia, is held every four years in honor of the goddess Hera. It consists of three running events for girls of different age groups.

---

1. Hill of Cronus.

2. Woods of Altis.

3. *Prytaneion*: houses the sacred fire used to light the fires on all the altars at Olympia.

4. Temple of Hera.

5. Treasuries of the Greek colonies.

6. *Gymnasium*: training area for running and throwing events.

7. *Palaestra* and baths: training area for jumping and wrestling events.

8. *Thokoleon*: seat of the Olympian priests.

9. *Leonidaion*: hotel for visiting dignitaries.

10. *Bouleuterion*: meeting place of the Olympic officials.

11. Temple of Zeus: houses the god's statue. One of the Seven Wonders of the World, the statue is made of ivory and gold, and stands over 43 feet tall.

12. Stadium, where all athletic events are held.

13. Athletes' tunnel entrance to the stadium (and cheats' list).

14. Hippodrome, where the chariot races are held.

15. River Alepheus (Alph).

The *Hoplite* Goes to War

The blare of trumpets, the early sun glittering on iron spears and bronze shields, the chants of war cries—all familiar sights and sounds to the people of Greece. The city-states battle each other for the slightest reason.

When a youth reaches the age of 20, his military training ends (*see pages 50–51*) and he is no longer an *ephebos*. Until he is 60 he will remain on the active service list, although men over 50 are sent into the reserves to be used in garrison duties.

Excepting Sparta, there are no professional standing armies. When a city goes to war, its citizens are called to the ranks, bringing their own equipment and provisions with them.

Development of the *hoplite*

The warlord and his retinue of aristocratic cavalrymen dominated armies before the Archaic Period, supported by a few poorly armed spearmen. While horses were expensive and only aristocrats could afford them, so was bronze armor and iron for swords, which meant few men could afford to be in an army.

In the Archaic Period (800-500 BCE), the city-states developed and armed militia were raised to defend their *polis*.

With increased trade, the middle classes began to prosper. They could now afford

good armor and weapons, and became heavily armed foot soldiers, known as *hoplites*. By the 7th century BCE, *hoplites* dominated the Greek army.

The call-up

The *ephebos* has finished his two years' military training; what can he expect as his city goes to war? At the call of his tribal *strategos* (general), he collects his military equipment—which his slaves have maintained in mint condition—and gathers with others of his *phyle* (tribe) at an appointed place. The state has not supplied him with any equipment because it is his honorable duty to provide all he needs to protect his fields, home, and family.

A man's wealth and social status determines the quality of his armor and weapons. As a result, he now stands in rank with fellow citizens whose armor type and quality varies considerably. Less wealthy citizens who cannot afford arms and armor are used as light infantrymen. Their function is to harass the enemy, screen the *hoplites*, and drive off other light troops.

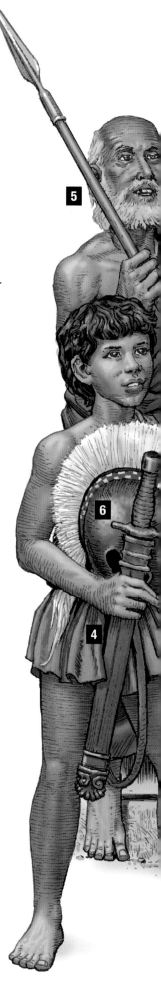

A *hoplite*'s equipment

1. A *hoplite*'s round shield is about 3 feet in diameter, large enough to protect his body from neck to thigh. It is made of bronze and toughened leather. Its outer surface is usually painted with the emblem of his city—an inverted V for Sparta, a gorgon's head (among other designs) for Athens, and the club of Hercules for Thebes.

2. The *hoplite* wears a linen cuirass, made of many layers of material glued together to form a stiff shirt 1/4 of an inch thick. From the waist down slits in the cuirass allow for easy movement, and a second layer of strips overlaps the outer to fill the vulnerable gaps.

3. Bronze leg guards, called *greaves*, protect his knees and shins.

Hoplite weapons are a straight, short iron sword (**4**) and a *sarise*—a long wooden thrusting spear tipped with an iron head, about 9 feet in length (**5**).

6. His helmet is made of bronze, usually from one piece of metal. Styles vary depending on the city, and they have changed over the years (*see panel opposite*).

Called to arms: Attended by his wife and family, an Athenian citizen *hoplite* prepares to go to war. He fastens a shoulder strap, while his eldest son proudly holds his helmet and sword ready. Clutching the spear, grandfather vividly recalls similar occasions in his own past, while the wife contemplates future dangers her sons will likely face.

On the march

The *hoplite* must also bring his own food. Typical rations include barleycorn, cheese, wine, and salted meat and fish. Servants or slaves accompany the army, carrying spare weapons and provisions for their masters, and cooking for them when fires are permitted. During a march, the *hoplite* straps his shield to his back, and clothing, bedding, or provisions can be tied to it, or hung from the end of his spear.

The Greeks march in long columns, with the horse-drawn baggage in the middle. If an attack is anticipated, they form a square to protect the baggage in the center.

Camps are established each night or when a battle seems imminent. These camps are rarely fortified, and troops sleep in formation, surrounding their supplies. Sentries are posted to warn of attack.

Helmets

Corinthian: An early style that made it difficult for the wearer to hear or see.

Illyrian: Made in two pieces joined at the crown with two protective ridges along either side of the seam.

Thracian and Attic: The later Thracian (left) and Attic (right) helmets offer good visibility. The Attic style will be adopted by Roman legionaries.

The Army in Battle

The most formidable army is that of Sparta. This *polis* is designed to support a permanent army, the best fighting force in Greece. Yet in battle, the *hoplites* of Athens are often the victors.

A Spartan soldier and his fallen Persian adversary. Spartans wear their hair long.

The Spartan army is organized differently from other Greek forces. The soldier lives with his comrades in barracks, not with his wife or family. The army is comprised of six *moroi* (battalion-sized units). A *mora*, commanded by a *polemarch*, is sub-divided into four *lochoi*. Each *lochos* (company) of 144 men is led by a *lochagos*, and under him four *entomarchs* command units of 36 men, known as *enemotia*.

The whole army is commanded by one of the Spartan kings. The first *mora* is the army's elite force and forms the king's bodyguard.

Spartans march into battle accompanied by *helots* (slaves), each carrying the armor and weapons of one soldier. Spartan soldiers are never expected to lose. If the unthinkable should happen, they will die fighting rather than retreat or surrender.

Athenian army organization

The Athenian army is formed by units from each of the ten tribes of Attica, which is why the word for "regiment" is the same as "tribe"—*phyle*. Of the ten *strategoi* (generals), only one or two are sent out into the field with each military expedition.

Sacrifices and religious services are a common aspect of campaign life, and omens are interpreted to predict the outcome of battles. Before fighting a battle, the *strategoi* meet to discuss how and where to fight, and sacrifices of livestock are offered to the gods to ensure victory.

In most cases, the army forms into a single line. The right wing of the line is the most vulnerable to a flanking attack because the soldiers at this end are partly unshielded (*see below*). Since the enemy will be aware of this weakness and attempt to exploit it, the most experienced units are posted on the right of the line.

The phalanx

Hoplites fight in a formation known as a phalanx, a block of soldiers of between eight and 12 ranks wide and more in depth. The men are armed with the *sarise* (spear), which turns a phalanx into a spiky battering ram.

When a soldier in the front line is killed or injured, the man behind him takes his place. The phalanx can also form into a formidable hollow square, defying any cavalry attack.

For the phalanx to be effective, the men must move as a unit. They use flute music to help keep in step. The man seen above playing the flute wears the Scythian apparel typical of Athenian archers.

On the charge, the first five ranks lower their 9-foot spears horizontally, projecting a lethal 6 feet ahead of the front rank.

The cavalry

Although *hoplite* foot soldiers form the bulk of the army, horsemen are useful as scouts and to break up enemy *phalanxes*. Each of the ten Athenian tribes is responsible for supplying one squadron of cavalry to a total force of a thousand men and horses. The cavalry is led by two commanders, called *hipparchs*, each in control of five squadrons.

When present, cavalry is either split between the two flanks or kept together as a mobile reserve and used to scatter enemy cavalry or light infantry that threatens to disrupt the line.

Auxiliary soldiers

Poor men who cannot afford the armor and weapons of a *hoplite* serve in lightly armed auxiliary units. They include archers, stone slingers, and *pilsoi*—men armed with clubs and stone maces.

The *peltast*

Peltasts are based on the principal troops of the Thracians, who found the combination of fighting and skirmishing abilities suited the rugged terrain of their homeland. The *peltast* is a light infantryman but he is also well armed.

Peltasts dash out from cover and hurl javelins into a *phalanx*, and then retreat. If a *phalanx* gets broken up, the *peltasts* go in and pick off individual *hoplites*. To counter the irritation of *peltasts*, fit, young *hoplites* called *ekdromoi* ("runners-out") run out of the *phalanx* to drive them off.

The Navy

Unlike the landlocked states of inland Greece, Athens bases her power mainly on her navy. The fast fighting ship of the fleet is the trireme, maneuverable and deadly in battle.

Triremes measure between 120 and 135 feet long, with a width of about 15 feet. The addition of an outrigger framework to support the oars increases the width by 2.5 feet on each side. They carry crews of up to 200 men, of whom 170 are oarsmen.

The remainder consists of 12–15 sailors, who man the sails or the steering oars, a similar number of marines (including about four archers), a flautist, whose rhythmic tones help the rowers keep in time, and the ship's commander, known as the *trierarch*.

The *trierarch* is usually a rich man, chosen by the state to pay for the running of the ship for one year, which indicates what an honor the role is for him. The same can be said for the oarsmen, free men and professional sailors mostly recruited from among the poorer citizens. However, in the time of war, even the elite are honored to man the oars of a Greek warship

Early Greek warships

The earliest—and smallest—type of long, low galley ship was the *pentaconter* (seen above, passing a cargo ship) powered by 25 oarsmen on either side. The ships described by Homer in his *Iliad* and *Odyssey* are biremes, galleys rowed by a hundred oarsmen, in two banks of 25 oars per side. Although fragile vessels, they were fitted with a projecting bronze beak for ramming enemy vessels. By the mid-6th century a third bank of rowers had been added to the typical warship, creating the trireme. By the end of the century the trireme had become the standard type of war galley in the eastern Mediterranean.

Three tiers of rowers

The rowers each use a single 14-foot long oar, and they are arranged in three banks, one above the other. On each side of the typical galley, 27 oarsmen known as *thalamites* form the lowest of the three tiers. These rowers place their oars through circular rowing ports.

The next tier of 27 oarsmen, *zygites*, sit above and slightly further outboard of the *thalamites*. Above them a top tier of 31 rowers, *thranites*, sit slightly outboard of the *zygites*, resting their oars on the outrigger frame.

Bulwarks (usually open at the upper level) protect the rowing benches, but above them the deck is partially covered, providing a broad fighting platform for *hoplites*, javelin men, and archers. A pair of helmsmen steer the trireme with a large oar at each side, However, the length and shape of the hull makes turning extremely slow, unless the oarsmen help in the maneuver by counter-steering on one side of the vessel.

In battle

Triremes use ramming tactics, rowing at speed into the flank of an enemy vessel to pierce its hull with a metal-tipped ram. When marines are carried, the *trierach* has the rare option to engage in boarding attacks. Otherwise, naval battles involve searching for a weak point in an enemy formation, then attacking, ramming, and sinking the ships.

A favorite tactic is to row at full speed toward the enemy ship, but swerve away at the last moment. The rowers on the side approaching the enemy vessel pull in their oars and the trireme glides past the enemy ship, breaking off its oars. The disabled ship can then be rammed and boarded.

Above: A battle between biremes. The prow (front) of the bireme and later trireme is equipped with a bronze or iron beak, used for ramming and sinking enemy ships.

Below: Ancient ships rarely sailed at night, the crew taking their meals and rest on the nearest shore.

No sailing at night

In ideal conditions, a trireme can travel under oars at about 10mph, but speeds are usually lower, due to fatigue, barnacle-encrusted hulls, and bad weather. A single central mast fitted with a simple square sail helps the rowers during long voyages, but both mast and sail are stowed before a battle

On long passages, the oarsmen work in two or three watches, or work periods so that they can get some rest. Triremes are unsafe in stormy weather, and there is no room onboard for the crew to cook or sleep, so most ships hug the coast and find a sheltered bay and beach for the night.

CHAPTER 5

Culture and Science

The Development of Literature and Thought

The Greek alphabet and writing system is the most sophisticated in the ancient world. The greatest achievements of the Greeks are made possible through the written word.

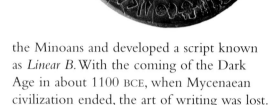

The earliest Greek writing system was developed by the Minoan culture of Crete. It was a form of hieroglyphic (picture) writing, which evolved by about 2000 BCE. By 1700 BCE, the Minoans had introduced a second script, known to us as *Linear A*. Some secrets of the hieroglyphs are understood, but *Linear A* remains a mystery.

By the 15th century BCE the Mycenaean Greeks had learned the art of writing from

Above: The Phaistos Disk (c.1600 BCE) is covered in signs representing a Minoan hieroglyphic script.

Detail of Mycenaean *Linear B* script. Experts can read it, but the clay tablets contain only lists of goods.

the Minoans and developed a script known as *Linear B*. With the coming of the Dark Age in about 1100 BCE, when Mycenaean civilization ended, the art of writing was lost.

When it was rediscovered in about 800 BCE, the new writing system came from the Phoenicians, a proper alphabet developed over centuries from Ugarit cuneiform, in turn descended from that of the Sumerians. However, the Phoenician alphabet contained only consonants and the Greeks extended it by adding vowels. The system was so successful that Greeks were able to create the most sophisticated literature of the time. The word *alphabet* is derived from the first two Greek letters, *alpha* and *beta*.

Lyrical poetry

The Greek alphabet and the development of writing made literary composition possible. The tales told by traveling poets of gods and Mycenaean heroes were the first stories to be written down. The most famous bard is Homer, who at some time about 850–750 BCE retold in writing the traditional stories of the Trojan War in his two epic poems, the *Iliad* and the *Odyssey*.

Written poetry was first read aloud by performers. Poetic recitations involved one or more performers. Poems were sometimes recited with dramatic flourish, and sometimes sung. A musical accompaniment of flute or lyre became common, leading to the development of large choral works, including religious odes, epitaphs for the dead, and songs of celebration. Music, singing, poetry, and prose eventually developed in the greatest cultural achievement of the Greeks—drama (*see pages 90–93*).

Left: Homer, the great storyteller.

The Greeks adapted the Phoenician form of the alphabet after the Dark Age.				
Phoenician		**Greek**		**Modern**
ALEPH	∢	ALPHA	A	A
BETH	𝄩	BETA	Β	B
GIMEL	⏌	GAMMA	Γ	C
DALETH	◁	DELTA	Δ	D
HE	⅄	EPSILON	E	E
VAV	Ⴘ			F
HETH	⊢	ETA	Η	H
TETH	⊕	THETA	θ	th
YOD	⅃	IOTA	I	I
KAPH	Ⴘ	KAPPA	K	K
LAMED	∣	LAMBDA	∧	L
MEM	⌇	MU	Μ	M
NUN	⅂	NU	N	N
SAMEK	≢	XI	Ŧ	x/ks
AYIN	O	OMICRON	O	O*
PE	𝄙	PI	Π	P
SADE	⌁			
KOPH	φ			Q
RESH	𝈚	RHO	Ρ	R
SHIN	W	SIGMA	Σ	S
TAW	Τ	TAU	Τ	T
		UPSILON	V	V
		PHI	Φ	f/ph
		CHI	X	X
		PSI	Ψ	ps
ZAYIN	I	ZETA	Z	Z
		OMEGA	Ω	O*

* Omicron represents a short "o" vowel sound, Omega a longer one.

Musicians accompany a poetry recital on this red-figured vase decoration.

Herodotus included first-hand accounts and personal memories. His *History* is not only the earliest example of pure Greek prose to survive, but also the world's first true history book.

Early prose

The Greeks were the first people to record their hopes, fears, and emotions in writing. Prose developed later than poetry. Philosophers, scientists, and historians used prose to clarify their search for truth through reasoned argument and observation. Later, prose became a vehicle for dramatic expression—the world's first novels.

Although designed for the middle and upper classes, they also show a sophistication of emotion and description that makes them timeless, and still relevant today.

Creating history

In the 5th century BCE, a series of Greek writers produced the world's first historical narratives, free from mythology, religion, and poetic license. Unlike other ancient histories, this Greek historical writing attempts to distinguish between fact and fiction and give straightforward accounts of human endeavor.

Herodotus is considered to be the father of modern history. He wrote his *History* in about 440 BCE, detailing the recent war between Greece and Persia.

In 404 BCE, the Athenian general Thucydides wrote a history of the Peloponnesian War between Athens and Sparta. He gives an impartial account of events, drawing on archived records, written statements, and first-hand accounts in a simple, direct, and concise style.

Thucydides died before the work was completed, but an Athenian nobleman named Xenophon finished it for him. Xenophon went on to write his own masterly *Anabasis* (up-country expedition), covering the campaigns of a Greek mercenary force against the Persians, culminating in the Battle of Cunaxa (401) and the retreat of the Greeks from Mesopotamia to the coast of the Black Sea.

The tradition established by these first Greek historians has provided modern historians with a scholarly and literary benchmark.

Above: Thucydides was a general in the Peloponnesian War, but his failure to relieve a besieged Athenian-held city in 424 BCE led to his ostracism (*see page 73*) from Athens. On his return in 404, he wrote his memoirs as the history of a soldier.

Xenophon's *Anabasis* was based on his own experiences as a soldier marching against the Persians. When the Greek leaders were betrayed and slain, Xenophon took command and brought the Greek forces safely home (**right**).

Philosophy and Medicine

Writing allowed philosophers to commit their arguments to paper. Through their clear, logical thinking, a new way of looking at the natural world has emerged, introducing rationality to the work of scientists, engineers, and doctors.

Pythagoras, famous for his theorem.

Philosophers are people who attempt to explain man's place in the scheme of things and how people should behave or what would be the ideal political system.

The basic elements

The first philosophers, Thales of Miletos, Anaximines, and Empedocles the Sicilian, argued about what substances were the most important in the composition of the universe—water, air, fire, or earth.

Pythagoras of Samos dominated the next generation of Greek philosophers. In about 531 BCE he moved to the Greek colony of Crotone in southern Italy, where he established a religious academy. Apart from

his famous mathematical theorem, Pythagoras advocated the portrayal of music as a mathematical exercise.

The next school of philosophers sprang up in Athens, when the statesman Pericles (c.495–429 BCE) befriended Anaxagoras. His pupils Democritus and Leucippus took the debate about life a stage further, when they argued that matter consisted of tiny atoms, two millennia before the concept would be taken seriously.

Socrates (469–399 BCE) questioned the accepted order of society, morals, and religion to such an extent that he was considered a menace. Sentenced to death, he elected to drink poison. Socrates was so modest that when the Oracle of Delphi pronounced him the wisest man in Greece, he replied that his wisdom stemmed from his acceptance that he knew nothing.

His greatest disciple, Plato (c.427–348 BCE), continued Socrates' methods, but

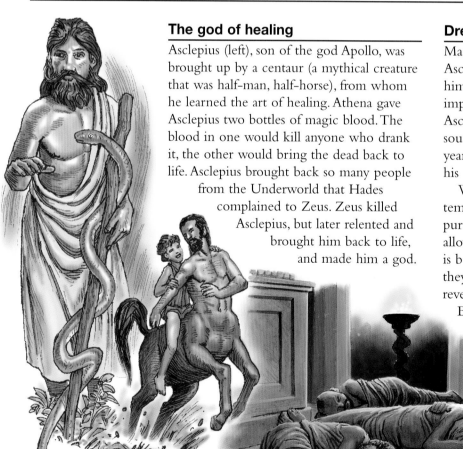

The god of healing

Asclepius (left), son of the god Apollo, was brought up by a centaur (a mythical creature that was half-man, half-horse), from whom he learned the art of healing. Athena gave Asclepius two bottles of magic blood. The blood in one would kill anyone who drank it, the other would bring the dead back to life. Asclepius brought back so many people from the Underworld that Hades complained to Zeus. Zeus killed Asclepius, but later relented and brought him back to life, and made him a god.

Dreams bring healing

Many Greek physicians are priests of Asclepius, and there are temples dedicated to him all over the Greek world. The two most important are at Athens and the sanctuary of Asclepius near the city of Epidaurus in the southeast of the Peloponnese peninsula. Each year a festival called the Epidauria is held in his honor at Athens.

When people fall ill, they visit one of the temples of Asclepius. After sacrifices and purification ceremonies, the sick person is allowed to sleep in the temple for a night. It is believed that Asclepius will heal them as they sleep, or appear to them in a dream to reveal what treatment would cure them.

By whatever means the cure is achieved, the recovered patient leaves Asclepius an offering as a tribute to the god and gift for curing them. This usually takes the form of a terracotta plaque showing the part of the person's body that has been made better by the divine intervention.

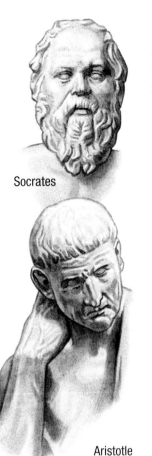

Socrates

Aristotle

exceeded his teacher's achievements through extensive writing. Plato tried to find the ideal way of governing a *polis* and set out detailed rules about how this could be done.

The Academy set up by Plato attracted some of the most prominent Athenians of the age, among whom was Aristotle (384-322 BCE). He was also interested in man and society and the ideal way to run a state, but had a wide knowledge of natural history. His most famous pupil was Alexander the Great.

In the 4th century BCE, Diogenes founded the school of philosophers known as Cynics. He lived very simply, and had no respect for the rules of society. He attacked dishonesty and excessive wealth. He lived so simply that at one point his home was a storage jar.

The most enduring of Greek philosophers were the Stoics, named after the *stoa* (porch) in Athens' marketplace where their founder Zeno (or Xenon, 344–262 BCE) founded the school of thought. He believed that if people acted naturally they would behave well, because the gods controlled their nature.

Alexander the Great asked if there was anything he could do for the great Cynic. "Don't stand between me and the sun," said Diogenes. Impressed by the reply, the king said, "If I were not Alexander, I should wish to be Diogenes."

Rational medicine

Following the example of philosophers, many doctors have adopted a more scientific approach to medicine and search for the rational causes of disease, and try to learn how the body works. For instance, it is believed that blood is the carrier of many common diseases, for which the remedy is to bleed the patient.

More commonly, these modern physicians prescribe herbal remedies, rest cures, special diets, and exercise. Surgery, however, remains a dangerous process and is usually avoided. Even when the patient survives the operation, infection often sets in and kills them.

The founder of this new medicine is

Hippocrates of Cos (460–377 BCE). He bases his medical practice on observation and rejects the popular view that illness is caused by possession of evil spirits or a punishment of the gods. Hippocrates teaches that the body must be treated as a whole and not just as a series of parts. He says that thoughts, ideas, and feelings come from the brain, and not the heart as other doctors believe.

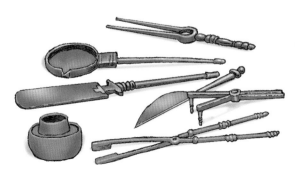

Hippocrates, seen here above, has separated practical medicine from religion. Through careful study of the workings of the human body, medicine is losing its elements of magic. Anatomy and inquiry play an ever larger role, as surgical skills and tools (**left**) steadily improve. Hippocrates uses treatments (**right**) according to his ability and judgment.

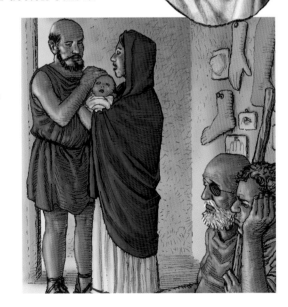

Scientists and Inventors

Rational thought as promoted by the Greek philosophers finds physical expression in the work of the many great minds who seek practical answers to solve problems.

To the Greeks, the study of philosophy goes beyond pondering the composition of the universe and the study of human nature. Scientists and engineers are also philosophers, which means "lovers of knowledge." By observing how things work, Greek philosophers are able to make many scientific discoveries.

Thales of Miletos (c.624–c.547 BCE) used mathematics to calculate the height of the Egyptian pyramids from a measurement of the length of their shadows. It is said that he was able to predict a solar eclipse, but he also claimed that the earth floats on water.

About the same time, Anaximines figured out that much of the planet had once been covered in water and humans had developed from an earlier creature (probably a fish).

The astronomer Aristarchus (310–230 BCE) realized that the earth revolves on its axis and circles the sun. Unfortunately, he did not have the evidence to prove it.

Anaxagoras (c.500–428 BCE) worked out that the moon's light is not its own but a reflection of the sun's. He also discovered that solar eclipses are caused by the moon passing between the earth and the sun, blocking out its light.

Archimedes (287–212 BCE), a native of Syracuse in Sicily, invented an easy and fast way to lift water from one level to another for irrigation, in the form of a large screw enclosed in a tube. Water is lifted by the screw as it is turned.

Archimedes was fascinated by the physical properties of water, and made his most famous discovery while taking a bath. He had filled the bath too full and when he sat in it, observed how the water rose up and overflowed. From this he realized that an object displaces its own volume of water.

Although levers have been in use since prehistoric times, Archimedes was the first scientist to explain the forces at work in leverage. He developed complex calculus in geometry, and also invented the most fearsome weapon of its day—the catapult.

The Greeks were the first to develop massive siege engines. Archimedes helped the Syracusans against Rome in 212 with many designs. This machine fired 6 foot-long arrows during the siege of Syracuse. The great scientist was killed by a Roman legionary after Syracuse finally fell in the same year.

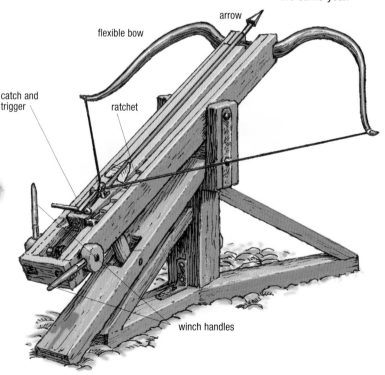

arrow

flexible bow

catch and trigger

ratchet

winch handles

Measuring distance accurately

Archimedes may have invented the *odometer*, a device that measures the distance traveled by a wheeled vehicle, which the Romans later used. It is described by a man named Vitruvius in about 27 BCE. A wheel of 4-foot diameter turns exactly 400 times in one Roman mile. For each revolution, a pin on the axle engages a cogwheel with 400 teeth, and so makes a complete revolution every mile. This engages another gear with holes around its circumference in which sit carefully graded pebbles. As it rotates, pebbles arrive over a tube, mile by mile, and drop into a counting box. The number of miles traveled is given simply by counting the number of pebbles that have dropped into the box.

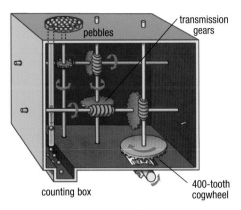

pebbles

transmission gears

counting box

400-tooth cogwheel

Aeolipile—the first steam engine

The *aeolipile*, or "wind ball," is a steam engine invented by a man named Heron, who lived in Alexandria in the 1st century AD. A sealed pot filled with water is placed over a flame and the water heated to boiling point. Two tubes rising from the top of the pot let the steam flow into a spherical metal ball. The globe, which is free to rotate on the inlet tubes, has two curved outlet tubes, which vent the steam. As the steam issues from the tubes, the metal sphere rotates. The *aeolipile* has no practical application; it is only an amusing toy.

The museum

The first museum is a Greek invention. In Alexandria there is a temple to the Muses, the nine goddesses who inspire and guide people's creative abilities, called the Museion. Scholars from all over the Greek world travel to study there. The Museion also houses a great library that contains copies of every important Greek book and many translations of foreign books.

Engineers working at the Museion have invented many interesting devices, although several—such as the *aeolipile* (*see above*)—have little functional use.

Telling the time with a water clock

For the Greeks measuring time is not a simple matter. Because the day (and night) is divided into a given number of periods (hours), it follows that throughout the year these periods vary in length between the longer summer days and shorter days of winter. Greek engineers overcome this problem by means of a *clepsydra*, or water clock. By altering the pressure on the inner cone, more or less water flows into the main chamber, altering the rate at which the cork float rises. In effect it allows the hours to go faster or slower for every day of the year.

The philosopher Plato is said to have invented a *clepsydra* with an alarm. Some water clocks are constructions of considerable size, requiring strong stone foundations, like this one at Athens.

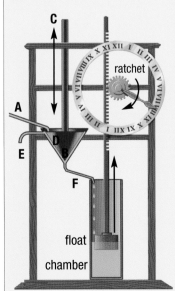

C

ratchet

A

D

E

F

float

chamber

A continuous supply of water enters the *clepsydra* by pipe **A**, filling the hollow cone **B**. By exerting pressure on lever **C**, solid cone **D** presses down on hollow cone **B**, restricting the water flow. Surplus water flows out through pipe **E**. Altering the pressure on the solid cone regulates the flow of water through pipe **F** into the chamber. This alters the rate at which the float rises, and the rate at which the ratchet turns the clock's hand. For clarity, Roman numerals are shown.

A Day at the Theater

In drama—the pinnacle of literature—the Greeks have invented a new art form. Going to the theater is a religious festival occasion and an entertaining day out.

Thespis was the first to write a play using an actor to speak a dialog exchange with the chorus on the "dancing floor."

Aeschylus, the father of modern theater.

Drama began as a countryside festival of the fertility god Dionysus. The first stages were the stone circles of a threshing floor (*see page 32*), where the oxen and mules "danced" over the cut wheat to separate the grain from the stalks. The threshing floor became the "dancing floor," or *orchestra* in Greek, and the natural place for honoring Dionysus with song and dance when the harvest was in.

The rural *orchestra* was always associated with a small stone altar for sacrifices and offerings, and nearby a small tent, or *skene*, which might be decorated to add a backdrop to the celebrations. From these humble beginnings grew the great Greek theaters of the 5th and 4th centuries BCE.

Rural rite to urban entertainment

The speed of transformation from a countryside celebration into a fully-fledged theatrical art form has been astonishing—approximately 85 years.

In about 530 BCE, the tyrant Peisistratus introduced a Dionysian festival at Athens, and an artist named Thespis wrote a few lines of dramatic dialog to be spoken between an orator and a Dionysian chorus on the *orchestra*.

Less than 50 years later in about 482, the dramatist Aeschylus (525–456) introduced the first written plays, involving troupes of no more than three masked actors.

And 40 years after that, construction began on the world's first purpose-built theater, on the lower slopes of the Acropolis of Athens, next to the Temple of Dionysus Eleutherus.

By this time—known as the Golden Age of Athens, under the leadership of Pericles—the dialog between the actors has become the most important part of the drama, with the chorus only commenting on the action. However, dramas remain religious in tone, since early productions were a combination of Dionysian worship and dramatic presentation.

The theater festival of Athens

The Dionysia is one of the city's most important religious celebrations. The festival, which lasts for five days, is a public holiday so that everyone can attend. The first day is devoted to processions and sacrifices. The following four days are taken up with drama competitions.

The man in charge of the Dionysia's organization is the *Eponymous Archon* (*see page 72*). He picks the wealthy citizens, called the *choregoi*, who have to pay for the production of the plays. These are presented in two distinct types—tragedies and

comedies, with a sub-division of tragedy known as a *satyr* play. Each year three tragedy writers and five comedy writers enter their plays into the contests.

Tragedies are usually about heroes of the Mycenaean past. The sweeping themes are grand, about human passions and conflicts, the misuse of power, and whether or not to bow to the will of the gods. After the earlier Aeschylus, the two most popular tragic writers are Euripides (484–406 BCE) and Sophocles (496–406 BCE).

Comedies feature ordinary folk, with commentaries on the politics and personalities of the day. They are bawdy, full of slapstick humor and rude jokes. The great master of comic writing is Aristophanes (448–c.380 BCE).

In the comedy competition, each author enters one play. However, in the tragic competition each author must enter three tragedies and a *satyr* play. This is a play that makes fun of the tragic theme (a style from which we get the term "satirical"). In a *satyr* play the people in the chorus dress as satyrs—the wild followers of Dionysus who were half-man and half-beast.

Euripides focuses on the common emotions and weaknesses of mankind. The audience can recognize something of themselves in his characters. The tragic finale often involves the actors subjecting their fate to the judgment of the gods, emphasizing the religious nature of Dionysian plays.

Fact box

From the name of Thespis, who wrote the first play with dialog, we derive the word "thespian," meaning actor.

"Drama" is a Greek word meaning "action."

The actors

Performers and chorus members are all men. Because of the flowing gowns and masks that hide their faces, the emphasis is on speech, not action. Tragic characters wear dark costumes, while comic figures wear bright colors. The actors' clothes are padded, and large wigs and thick-soled shoes are worn, to make actors easily seen in the huge theaters.

Masks

Actors wear painted masks of stiffened fabric or cork. The expressions show the character's age, gender, and feelings. By switching from a "happy" to a "tragic" mask, an actor can change mood instantly. A performer can even change roles by swapping masks. The expressions are greatly exaggerated to make them visible, even from the back of the theater. The large open mouths also act as amplifiers for the actors' voices.

Below: The comic plays of Aristophanes are the talk of Athens. They contain attacks on the pompous nature of Athenian officials. He uses much more action on the stage than other playwrights, catchy music and lyrics, funny recitations, and enjoyably farcical plots. His humor is irreverent, democratic, and hugely popular.

Above: The superb characterization employed by Sophocles fires the imagination of theatergoers. A master of dramatic tension, he brings his plays to explosive conclusions that thrill the audience.

Inside the theater

The *koilon* (or later *theatron*, "a place of seeing") is built in a half-circle of rising stone seating. The blocks of seats are called *cavea*. The *proedria*—the first (and lowest) row of seats—is reserved for senior figures in the *polis*, visiting dignitaries, or for priests. They are much more comfortable than the ordinary benches for everyone else, but—whether distinguished or ordinary—spectators usually bring something soft to sit on because the stone seating takes its toll on the hardiest backside!

A raised platform, known as the *logeion*, allows actors to stand over the proceedings, watching events on the *proskenion* as if from afar, and the entire stage is covered with a flat roof called the *theologeion*. Rushes dipped in a sulfurous solution can be lit to create dramatic light and smoke effects. The *aeorema* (crane), permits actors to "fly" onto the *skene*, usually those playing the part of a god. The *ekeclema* is a wheeled platform for presenting or removing "dead" characters. This is often used in tragedies for showing the audience characters who have been killed off-stage. A pair of revolving *periaktoi* (triangular pillars, not shown) can be turned to present a new item of scenery and remove an old one.

koilon or
theatron
with
blocks of
cavea

aeorema
ekeclema
theologeion
skene
logeion
proskenion
parados
orchestra
themili
proedria

The people from each deme of the *polis* have their own block of seats. Tokens are used as tickets, the letters on them indicating which block of seats the token-holder can sit in. The seats are not expensive, but the state pays for poor people.

A theater's main elements

Theaters in Greece share certain features. Almost all are composed of three major elements: the *orchestra* (chorus space), the *koilon* (auditorium), and the *skene* (backdrop, from which we derive the word "scene"). Most action takes place on a raised platform, or *logeion*. The *orchestra* is a circular, oval, or sometimes rectangular space in front of the *logeion*. The *orchestra* houses the chorus, with its director—known as the *koryphaios*—standing on a *themili* (originally the small Dionysian altar of the threshing floor).

Although the *logeion* is the main stage, actors tend to perform on its forward edge, known as the *proskenion* ("in front of the skene"). The sides and rear of the stage are decorated with painted panels, or even permanent walls, which hide actors standing off stage from the audience. These backdrops set the scene with depictions such as wooded glades or mountaintops.

Between the *skene* and the audience seated in the *koilon*, there are two walkways known as the *paradoi* (entrance ways). The chorus enters through one *parados* in solemn procession at the play's start, and actors enter the theater through them, speaking or singing as they walk on.

Symbolism is important. An actor arriving on the *skene* from the left is deemed to have come from the countryside, while one arriving on the right has come from the sea or a city. Behind the *proskenion*, two symbolic doors allow actors to enter and exit the action, moving through them from the *proskenion* to the rear of the stage, or *logeion*, where they are considered to be still in scene, but not directly participating in it.

Bringing the past to vivid life

Principally, the Greek theater is a place of religious celebration. But in its comedies and tragedies, its satire and political comment, its emotions and ambitions, Greek drama portrays the everyday lives of ordinary as well as extraordinary people of the time.

Glossary

acropolis The key point of a city, usually at the top of ("akro" in Greek) a hill.

adyton A small area within a temple where only priests and oracles can go.

agora An open space near a town's center. Originally just a marketplace, an agora is also a place to hold political meetings.

andron The part of a building where only men are allowed (so, dining room). See also *gynaeceum*.

archons The nine chief magistrates, different offices of archons given different tasks. Old archons become members of the **Areopagus**, a council of elders.

aristoi The "best people" of Greece—aristocrats or nobles.

black-figure A type of pottery decoration with black figures set against the undecorated red of the vessel. *Red-figure* pottery was more popular by the 6th century BCE.

Boule The governing council of a *polis*. Athens' Boule has 50 members from each of the ten *phylae*, but the size and influence of a council varies from city to city. They meet in a **Bouleuterion**.

cella The rectangular main room in the center of a temple that holds a statue representing its god.

chiton A square robe of wool or linen, fastened at one side with **fibulae** (pins).

deme Within a *polis*, a semi-independent district, village, or small town and its people. Each has a demarchos, or mayor.

demos The people of a district, from which the word democracy—rule by the people—is derived.

Dorians People from northern Greece who populated central Greece and the *Peloponnese* by c.1000 BCE, replacing *Mycenaean* civilization.

ekklesia Known in English as the Assembly and the **apella** at *Sparta*, every free man is allowed to vote at its public meetings, held a few times per month.

Eleusis A district near Athens where secrets are revealed to initiates of the Mysteries festival, held in honor of the corn goddess Demeter and her daughter Kore.

epheboi Male youths aged 18–20 who are given military and religious training.

Gerousia *Sparta's* council of elders, elected for life from among the *aristoi*.

gymnasium A place of exercise, particularly for *epheboi* in military training. Areas and buildings for education and philosophical debate were added to the **palaestra**, the courtyard exercise area.

gynaeceum The female quarters of a building, where only women are allowed. See also *andron*.

helots A type of slave known from *Sparta*, where they belong to the state rather than individual owners.

Hellenization The spread of Greek culture, from the Greeks' word for themselves, Hellenes, which itself came from the name Hellas, a region of *Thessaly*.

herm A stone pillar topped with a bust of a god—usually Hermes, the messenger god—set within a city to mark a crossroads or boundary, outside a home for luck, or between towns as a milestone.

hetairai Women specially educated in the fields of art, philosophy, and politics and skilled in music and poetry. They are the only women allowed at a *symposium*. Male companions are called **hetairoi**.

himation A woolen cloak. A **chlamys** is a short cloak for men, pinned at the right shoulder.

hoplite A heavily armed infantryman. Hoplites formed into **phalanxes**, each soldier's shield also helping to defend a neighbor.

hydria A jar for holding water, with two side handles for carrying and a larger vertical one for pouring.

kitharistes A music teacher, who plays the **kithara**, a seven-stringed instrument which was a forerunner of the guitar.

krater A large vase or bowl for diluting wine, which is then transferred to an *oinchoe* for pouring.

kyrios The head of a household. They are always men and are the guardians of any females in the home.

Metics People foreign to a *polis*, whether from a different country or just another city-state. They were not full citizens so could not vote.

metropolis Literally "'mother city,"

a *polis* on the Greek mainland that has colonies overseas.

Minoan A 3rd–2nd century BCE civilization of the island of Crete, named after the legendary King Minos. It spread elsewhere around the Aegean Sea but faded after the palace of Knossos was destroyed c.1400 BCE.

Mycenaean A Greek civilization beginning c.1600 BCE, named after Mycenae city in the northeastern *Peloponnese*. Mycenaean culture declined during Greece's Dark Age, c.1100, when the *Dorians* invaded.

oinchoe A wine jug; wine is often mixed with honey and called **oinomelo**.

Olympians Greece's sky gods, ruled by Zeus on Mount Olympus.

oracle A woman believed to tell the future. In myth and reality, men made offerings at oracles' temples and asked questions via priestesses who uttered the oracles' replies.

paedogogus A servant or slave who supervises or gives a child's education.

Peloponnese The peninsula of southern Greece, with the Ionian Sea on its west and the Aegean Sea on its east. It is separated from northern Greece by the Gulf of Corinth.

peltast A type of light infantryman armed with a spear and shield.

peplos A long, tubular robe worn by women.

Persia A Middle Eastern country whose Achaemenid dynasty invaded then ruled Egypt from 525 BCE. Athens and *Sparta* defeated Persian invasions of Greece in 490 and 479.

Phoenicians People from the western shore of Asia, around what is now Lebanon. In earlier times they were known as Canaanites and ruled by the Egyptians in the 15th–13th centuries BCE.

phratria A group of local families, derived from the word "phrater" (brother). New children were accepted into their phratria in October's Apatouria gathering. There are several *phratriai* in each *phyle*.

phyle A division of a *polis's* population, based on the status and number of members. Athens had ten phylae, each phyle containing one **trittye**—a group of *demes*—from each of the three zones (city, inland and shore).

polis A city, or a city and its surrounding area also called a city-state.

propylon "Before the gate"—a grand gateway, usually to a sacred site or a palace.

prytani A committee of 50 men drawn from one *phyle*, the prytani changing at regular intervals to give each *phyle* equal importance.

red-figure A type of pottery decoration with clay-red figures set against the painted black of the vessel. Decorative vessels went out of fashion in the 4th century BCE.

Sacred Way The path in a religious complex such as Delphi that leads from its entrance, winding its way through subsidiary structures, to its principal temple.

sophists Scholars who travel from place to place, giving lectures and offering tutorship on various subjects. Philosophers accused them of encouraging argument.

Sparta A military state established by *Dorians* in the southern *Peloponnese*. In contrast to Athens and other city-states, it was ruled by kings (two ruling at the same time) and gave women almost equal rights. Male citizens entered military training at the age of 7 and became *hoplites*, served by *helots*.

stoa A generally long building with rooms opening onto a colonnaded walkway. Also called a porch, some have a second story.

strategos A military general, who commands on both land and sea.

symposium An evening feast for men usually held in the *andron*, including entertainment, debate, and the drinking of much wine.

Titans The elder, earth gods led by Cronus, overthrown by Zeus who began the new rule of sky gods, the *Olympians*.

Trojan War A mythical conflict between the Greeks and the city of Troy, in retaliation for Prince Paris's abduction of Helen, beautiful wife of King Menelaus of *Sparta*. As told in Homer's epic poem, the *Iliad*, the war lasted nine years, until the Greeks presented Troy with a hollow horse, from which soldiers conquered the city.

Underworld The realm of the dead, ruled by Hades and guarded by Cerberus, a three-headed dog.

Index